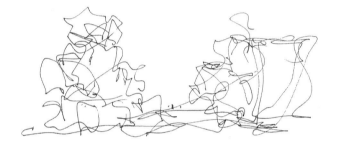

BUILDING STATA

The Design and Construction of Frank O. Gehry's Stata Center at MIT

Nancy E. Joyce   Commentary by Frank O. Gehry   Photographs by Richard M. Sobol

The MIT Press   Cambridge, Massachusetts   London, England

Printed and bound in the United States of America by Quebecor World/Kingsport.

Library of Congress Cataloging-in-Publication Data

Joyce, Nancy (Nancy Eleanor)
  Building Stata : the design and construction of Frank O. Gehry's Stata Center at MIT / Nancy E.
Joyce ; commentary by Frank O. Gehry ; photographs by Richard M. Sobol.
     p.   cm.
  Includes index.
  ISBN 0-262-10105-X (hc. : alk. paper); 0-262-60061-7 (pbk. : alk. paper)
  1. Massachusetts Institute of Technology—Buildings—Design and construction. 2. Ray and
Maria Stata Center for Computer, Information, and Intelligence Sciences (Cambridge, Mass.)
I. Gehry, Frank O., 1929–   II. Title

  T171.M8195J69 2004

Picture Credits

Boston Globe (staff produced copy only) by Globe Staff Graphic/David Butler. Copyright 2003 by Globe Newspaper Co (MA).
Reproduced with permission of Globe Newspaper Co (MA) in the format Other Book via Copyright Clearance Center., page 74
Gehry Partners, pages i, 17–19, 24 (right), 25 (left), 26–37, 40–44, 46–47, 49–51, 54–69, 133
Haley & Aldrich, Inc., pages 81, 84–85
Image Archives of the Historical Map & Chart Collection/Office of Coast Survey/National Ocean Service/NOAA, page 5
Library of Congress, Geography and Map Division, Washington, D.C., page 4
MIT Dept. of Electrical Engineering and Computer Science Archive, pages 2–3
Courtesy MIT Museum, pages 6, 9–13, 15, 16 (bottom), 21
Judith Nitsch Engineering, Inc., page 45 (left)
Olin Partnership, page 45 (right)
Skanska USA Building Inc., pages 38–39, 48 (top; bottom right), 84 (top, center, and bottom left), 85 (top, center, and bottom right), 95 (right)
Richard M. Sobol, pages ii–v, viii–xv, 16 (top), 24 (left), 25 (right), 48 (bottom left), 70–73, 75–80, 82–83, 86–94, 95 (left), 96–131, 138
Wallace Floyd Design Group, page 20; model photograph by Sam Sweezy, page 22
Wilfried Kramb, pages 52–53
www.mapsovertime.com, page 7

The vision for this building—for any building—evolves. I don't start out with a preconception. I'm looking for interaction, getting the client to collaborate with me so that the building will be as much theirs as mine. I am the person who interprets their needs into some kind of form.

The building I'm going to make is going to fit into the neighborhood, have human scale, engage the people, make them want to go there and be excited to be associated with it. What I want to do is make some kind of magic and take people someplace they've never been before—someplace that they would like to go to in the end, when the building is complete.

COMMENTARY

Frank O. Gehry

I try to separate from the business component and use my own private space for the creative work. I do a lot of my sketching at home. Usually, at home, I'll sit and think about the project and sketch when nobody is around. Sometimes, if I can't get to sleep, I'll draw.

Am I able to visualize what happens? Well, in the design phase, when I am looking at the models, I have an intuition that sets things in motion. It's like a ripple effect— when you throw a rock into water, the ripples go out. I am confident that those ripples are going to be what they ultimately become. Not that I know exactly each and every picture, but I follow the details of the materials.

I do sketches and then we develop a direction. It depends on whom I am working with. You cannot find the point where Frank Gehry ends and Gehry Partners begins. It's pretty seamless all the way to the end.

We study the models a lot. When we make a specific element on a model, we are trying to break down the scale and shift the scale of the pieces in order to avoid its becoming big and monolithic. Like the horizontal break on the Gates Tower— that's there to break down the scale.

That's why we do two scale models. If you do only one, then the model becomes the object and you lose perspective on the building. Also, without the two models it becomes really difficult to get across to the client what we are aiming for.

When it's all done, this is going to fit in its context pretty nicely. I was worried that, when you see shapes like this, you might think it looks like something from a cartoon. Some of the early models scared me and some others who saw them; I agonized a lot about that. Then a colleague said to me that the building is "Leger-like," which is a great compliment. I love Leger, so that gave me confidence and a clue. And, in reality, it's not a cartoon at all. It is much tougher and more anchored.

I made models of all those windows so I knew where I liked them and where I didn't. Once we saw them in the models, some of them we pushed in or out a little more.

To find creative solutions within the context of the reality of budgets, that's what hones you. You constantly value engineer your ideas and make choices. The choices are the honing of the ideas to the finale. That goes on all the way to the end of the project. And there are always things you may have wanted, but then you value engineer them and you come up with new schemes.

I like to stay on schedule. I think that, in the end, all these budget disciplines and time disciplines can be worked to your advantage if you don't allow them to intimidate you. Some people get intimidated and then they are bound to fail because they see it as an obstacle course instead of the reality of the amount of work involved.

Academia functions kind of like a bureaucracy, where time deadlines and constraints aren't the crisis issues they are for us. If we miss a deadline, it's going to cost us because nobody is going to pay extra. Academics should try it—dreaming up creative stuff, coming up with out-of-the-box thinking under pressure. We don't let the clients just sit back and listen to us. That would never be my way of dealing with the world. We draw them into it. MIT might not have gotten into the process otherwise.

There are about a hundred people who shaped this with us. I take energy from listening to the client to make the things that we do. I argue with them and try to give them things to upset them and get them excited and do all kinds of things just to push the envelope. I love that process—even more than the finished building. In the end, the people mean more to me. You know, I have designed buildings that I have never been to because the people I worked with weren't there at the end, so I didn't go see them.

In the interiors of Stata, now, we have a fairly open system and the people in the building can move stuff around and they don't have to call us. They don't have to feel that it's precious. It won't feel precious. It is simple now and it's going to be simple in a couple of years. If anybody wants to move they can just go to the store, buy three sheets of plywood, and nail it up, finish it and they've got it.

I think of this in terms of controlled chaos. I always relate it to democracy. Democracy is pluralism, the collision of ideas. Our cities are built on a collision of thought. Look out there. There is a building by Pei, there is a bridge, there is that huge hunk in the distance. If it wasn't for democracy it would all look like one thing. Stata represents that idea, which I think is where we are in life now.

For some time I have been fascinated with the Morandi paintings of bottles—how separate pieces touching breaks down the scale. For the Stata Center, we took that idea much further. You have the same building, essentially one building, and it looks like ten buildings. If you look at the connections between the parts—where each "bottle" touches the next—it looks like one building, but there are ten. That's how we went about keeping it from seeming gargantuan and cold.

The building reflects the culture of the groups inside it. They are all going to be colliding with each other intellectually over time. That's what gives it strength. That's what it's all about. It's unpredictable. For the rest of their lives here they are going to discover things because of nature. The sun and the light change and when they do, with these cracks and spaces where light comes in, that's going to change the people. There are going to be some miracles here.

I am happy that this building expresses what's going on inside. My interpretation is that it reflects the different groups, the collision of ideas, the energy of people and ideas. They each have their own sorts of vectors and they will all be colliding with each other, some accidentally and some by contrivance. That's what will lead to the breakthroughs and the positive results. I think that's really going to work. I can't wait to see everybody in there—to see the beehive buzzing.

We push the trades. Skanska and Cannon will go out and use CATIA from now on. They got trained here. Some of the trades are open minded and view this as a real chance to go to the next level. There will be tremendous change in the construction industry and we are way at the head of it.

Preface

In 1990, I was privileged to come to MIT to serve as its fifteenth president. I found at MIT the most vital, energetic, creative, intense, and disciplined intellectual community imaginable. The whole place glows, hums, inspires, and excites. But two things bothered me—the planform of the campus and its backdoor. From the top floors of the adjacent Marriott Hotel, I could look down on MIT and see an unbroken rectilinear layout that somehow instantly made me think more of a naval base than of a campus for such a wonderful academic community. I also confess to a depressed feeling upon driving down the tired, treeless Vassar Street at the back of the primary campus, where steam plants, decaying buildings, and the nearly dilapidated and dismal gray-shingled Building 20 flanked the street. This was MIT's backdoor—its northern edge.

The south side of MIT's campus, however, is spectacular. Here's where you encounter MIT's iconic image, the great buildings designed by Welles Bosworth and constructed on the banks of the Charles River in the early years of the twentieth century. The bold scale and concept, classical in form, of this new beaux arts campus must have seemed incongruous as a home for electric generators, steam engines, and the apparatus of industrial chemistry that would define the coming age of technology.

And if the dome and columns of Bosworth's Building 10 reflect our public image, Building 20 contained much of our soul. Constructed as a temporary facility during World War II, Building 20 was home to part of the MIT Radiation Laboratory. Within the wood and asbestos "RadLab," scientists and engineers took the British invention of radar and developed it into devices and systems that contributed immeasurably to the Allied victory. By century's end, Building 20 had been home to a five-decade procession of unprecedented intellectual adventure, radical invention, fascinating people, hands-on learning, and irreverent, world-changing thought.

On the threshold of a new century and millennium, MIT had the responsibility of razing Building 20 and constructing in its place a new home for computer, information, and intelligence sciences. Although we carefully assessed a wide range of architects and concepts, everyone involved in the decision recognized that this could be no ordinary building. MIT needed to be as bold at the start of the twenty-first century as our predecessors had been at the start of the twentieth. The time had come to build a facility, the physical form of which signaled the intellectual brashness, energy, and excellence held within. This building must display our soul as well as contain it.

Above all others, this building needed to be adventurous in its exterior appearance. It would house a group of faculty known for the importance and innovation of their work. And it would stand at a critical location that announced our campus and set it off from the immediately surrounding, densely commercial area.

Are Frank Gehry and MIT "making a statement" with the exuberant, joyous architecture of this building? I think the statement is that MIT is a bold and confident institution, a place where people do very important, profound work yet do not take themselves too seriously.

The conceptualization, significance, and vision of the Ray and Maria Stata Center evolved over time, and not without risk. For over thirteen years, the highest-priority capital request of the School of Engineering had been a new building to bring the Laboratory for Computer Science and the Artificial Intelligence Laboratory back from rented commercial space in Technology Square, returning it to the heart of our academic campus. By 1997, we had a basic program for the building and important early financial pledges had been secured from two dedicated and accomplished alumni, Ray Stata and Alex Dreyfoos, and from Microsoft founder Bill Gates, who admired LCS director Michael Dertouzos and whose company had benefited greatly from MIT graduates, ideas, and technology. So we decided to move forward and select an architect.

A committee of Electrical Engineering and Computer Science Department faculty, MIT planners, and key facilities department leaders established and implemented a process to request and screen proposals from a range of architectural firms. The guidance of Bill Mitchell, dean of MIT's School of Architecture and Urban Planning and architectural adviser to the president, was important and effective.

In due course, the committee narrowed the selection to a choice between two outstanding architects, whose styles were quite different. Frank Gehry clearly was the more adventurous of the two. I met with the committee and gave each of its members the opportunity to state his or her preference and their reasoning behind that choice. Precisely half the group favored Gehry, so I had to make a decision.

A few evenings later I walked home and told my wife that I had just made a momentous decision, one for which I would be either admired or vilified in the future. MIT was going to take a huge step into a very different world of architecture. I knew this entailed risk, but my confidence had been affirmed by Bill Dickson, our senior vice president, a man of strong pragmatism and wisdom. I figured that if I could get him to agree with the bold move of giving the commission to Frank Gehry, I could have confidence that we were doing the right thing. After some discussion, he concurred and, indeed, tipped the scale by relating how radical the design of our beautiful, elegant Kresge Chapel had been considered when it was started in 1953.

After Dickson had informed Gehry that MIT wanted him to design this important facility, I called him to reinforce the importance of this project to our campus, especially in its replacement of Building 20, which, despite its total unsightliness, had played a profound role in our academic history. As we talked, my concern about risk dissipated. It was clear that Frank Gehry already had a deep understanding of MIT and what we wanted to do. The fact is, we spent much of the time sharing tales about the late Caltech scientist Richard Feynman, an incredibly brilliant and colorful physicist who had been a student at MIT. Clearly, Gehry was an "MIT person."

The program evolved as we thought more about the Stata Center's role in the life of the campus. It became clear that we needed to construct a large parking structure beneath the complex in order to preserve precious surface space and enable smooth functioning in the Northeast Sector of our urban campus. The Stata Center also became the home of the Department of Philosophy and Linguistics, and a long-needed major child-care facility was added, helping to make MIT a more attractive place to work.

Further, the project presented an important opportunity to provide a large, appealing, student-oriented area with first-rate classrooms and space for students to gather, ponder, converse, and relax between classes. Such space has been in low supply in MIT's academic buildings, and creating more of it is consistent with our agenda to improve the quality of student experience beyond the classroom and laboratory. In essence, the Student Street Gehry fashioned became a manifestation of the new spirit called for in 1998 by MIT's Task Force on Student Life and Learning.

The success of Frank Gehry's Ray and Maria Stata Center for Computer, Information, and Intelligence Sciences can be judged fully only many years hence. The most important criteria should be the traditional ones: Did the building support world-class research? Was it a place that faculty and staff enjoyed coming to each day throughout their careers? Has it adapted to the ever-changing needs and research modalities of world-leading academic units? Were we able to maintain the building physically with relative ease and at a reasonable cost? Was its balance of comfort level with energy and utility use appropriate? Did its classrooms enable faculty and students to go about the business of teaching and learning effectively and efficiently? In short, is it a great place to teach, study, work, and conduct research?

But other criteria for success are specific to the special nature of this building, and how well they have been met will be apparent within its first few years. Does the Student Street raise the spirits of the young men and women who learn, meet, and commune along it? Do the building's occupants occasionally discover new views, perspectives, images, forms, or patterns that intrigue, challenge, or simply provide them with enjoyment or amusement? Do people think about elements or spaces and ask themselves, "Why did Frank Gehry do this?"—and do they have an inkling of the answer? Does the Center inspire us and open our thinking? Is it a suitable icon for our distinguished Department of Electrical Engineering and Computer Science? Does it enhance and reflect the evolving culture of MIT?

As the MIT community became aware of Gehry's design, a tension became evident. Engineers, especially those of my generation or earlier, tend to be pragmatic, frugal, and perfectly at home within rectilinear offices and laboratories with cinderblock walls. I respect that. So it was no surprise to find that the renderings of Gehry's design were frequently met with skepticism or incredulity. But as the design has been transformed into a real physical structure and people have seen its actual form and scale, many skeptics have been converted. Once the interior is experienced, most remaining doubt will be converted to enthusiasm. Of course, not all such questions will or should disappear because the Stata Center is intended to stir imagination and invite strong views.

The most frequently asked question during design and construction was, "Will the Center stand the test of time?" In my view, it almost certainly will, but not as a "timeless" structure. It will always be obvious when it was built and who designed it. And I think we will be proud of that.

—*Charles M. Vest*

Foreword

It is a wonder that I find myself writing about the Ray and Maria Stata Center. I came to MIT in 1979 as a young, new faculty member in chemical engineering, drawn to MIT by its clear definition of excellence, its national and international reputation in science and engineering, and by the combination of creativity and precision in research and education it fostered. But most of all, I was attracted to the image of the Institute as an academic world leader, which I measured in terms of the Institute's standing in academic disciplines and in pioneering research.

Eighteen years later I found myself at the center of a critical process for MIT that had little to do with any of my previous professional experience. It was through this position that I fully came to understand the place of leadership in a complex institution. As the relatively new dean of engineering, I was the owner of the building project that would bring the computer science

faculty, staff, and students of the Department of Electrical Engineering and Computer Science (EECS) back to campus, after more than forty years in off-campus rental space. The site of the new building was in an MIT outback called the Northeast Sector, which was defined by parking lots, garages, and the decaying Building 20.

What I first naively imagined to be the straightforward programming and design of an academic building evolved into a much more complicated journey that, in the end, challenged the very culture of MIT. Previously, new laboratory building projects followed long-prescribed methods of massing—usually a double-loaded single-corridor design. Moving away from this required innumerable discussions, consensus building, and difficult decisions.

The opportunity posed by the new building on this particular site was much larger than simply constructing facilities that would house several academic laboratories and

centers. The site itself is at the center of twenty-first-century MIT. You can see this simply by reviewing the neighbors to the Stata Center: biology, chemical engineering, biological engineering, physics and electrical engineering, and computer science compose the umbrella of disciplines that surrounds the Stata Center. Today, more than half of all MIT undergraduates are enrolled in one or more of these departments. Indeed, the Stata project's original objective—to bring the Laboratory for Computer Science (LCS) and the Artificial Intelligence Laboratory (AILab) back to campus—would warm the intellectual heart of any engineering dean because of the centrality of computer science and information technology to the evolution of engineering and science going forward. Communications research in the Laboratory for Information and Decision Systems (LIDS) and Linguistics and Philosophy make great neighbors in the building, as first envisioned by Joel

Moses, the previous dean of engineering, who was the provost when the project was launched. The idea of adjacency of these academic units was well motivated and intellectually straightforward. That is where the simplicity of the project ended.

Frank Gehry saw the complexity and the opportunity posed by the program of the new building and its presence on the campus. During the early master-planning exercise, Frank invited us to expand our goals for the project beyond our original conception. During these early meetings, three themes quickly emerged as dimensions by which the success of the Stata Center would ultimately be judged.

First, and absolutely essential, was the creation of space for the faculty, students, and staff who would occupy the Stata Center. The client described a hierarchical organization that required spaces ranging in accessibility, from the totally open areas shared by members of a community to private offices for individual faculty members. The need to balance these competing desires became an underpinning of the Stata Center design.

The second theme was the opportunity to open the MIT campus with a new face in a new direction. When I came to MIT, the corner of Vassar and Main was a wasteland that was little changed in 1997! But the promise of a landscape of vibrant research and industrial neighbors was already there: the Whitehead Institute for Biomedical Research occupied the southeast corner of the Vassar and Main intersection and the first of the biotechnology companies had begun moving into the neighborhood. It was not hard to imagine that the Stata Center could replace the back-lot atmosphere of Building 20 and a decaying parking garage with a new, iconic face for this side of MIT. With completion of the Stata Center, the new Brain and Cognitive Sciences Center designed by Charles Correa and Goody Clancy across Vassar Street, and the logos of several new pharmaceutical and biotechnology companies becoming visible on nearby buildings, a new entrance to MIT is being created.

The third theme, place for communities, emerged during the evolution of the design and, in the end, may be one of the most successful elements of the project. The Stata Center gave MIT much more than the simple opportunity to move the computer science faculty back to MIT. The programming and design of the center spelled the opportunity to create space that would define communities at MIT. No spaces for this type of integration existed in this portion of the campus.

Which communities? The number grew as programming proceeded. We expanded from the original list of academic units—departments, laboratories, and centers, which are collections of single faculty members and their research groups—to the entire student body, faculty, and staff of MIT, and finally to the Cambridge community at large, with the Stata Center serving as a new campus gateway to the northeast. Developing a client committee and a program that would represent all these communities was the first challenge. MIT was incredibly fortunate to have Christopher Terman of EECS to head the client group and Nancy Joyce as project manager for the Stata Center Project. With their leadership, the client's voice was clearly and systematically heard throughout the process.

Another challenge was presented by the site itself. The expansion of MIT along Vassar Street had long been imagined as yet another of the rectangular bar buildings positioned between the street and the aging but historically significant Alumni Pool. Although the site seemed large at first, its shape and the need for separation from the pool severely constrained the massing of elements in the building, forcing a linear orchestration that would result in separation of people and communities.

The genius of Frank Gehry's design is in turning the variety of communities and the constraints of the site into a powerful statement about MIT's campus and about the integration of communities. Frank pushed us to realize the potential for the Northeast Sector of campus. He also pushed us to expand the program to include the kinds of spaces that would be inviting to the larger parts of the MIT community. We did this by including teaching and public space, a much-needed child-care facility—luckily, we were already armed with a wonderful report from my faculty colleagues about the desperate need for this facility—and food services, the great magnet on a university campus. The final piece was to rest the center on a large underground garage and service facility.

As provost, starting in 1998, I was in a position where I needed to speak for the entire academic community and therefore generate a consensus for the expanded program for the Stata Center with other leaders at MIT. This was not hard. The lack of community space was acknowledged as was the need for new common facilities, and the background already in place, thanks to the report of the Task Force on Student Life and Learning, highlighted the need for community spaces for the undergraduate population.

Frank Gehry and the client committee did the rest. After several iterations, Frank produced a design concept that filled the space between Vassar Street and the Alumni Pool and that created layers of communities that are visually connected but physically distinct. He created topography where none existed and allowed the Stata Center to envelop the Alumni Pool with a purpose by integrating new athletic facilities adjacent to the pool as part of the community commons in the Center. The terrace of green space, almost at pool-top level, is a modern version of an academic cloister, although a radically different one because it is inverted. The crescent formed by the Gates and Dreyfoos Buildings shelters this space from northern exposure, but not from the rest of the academic environment; instead, the space is raised and exposed, welcoming the community into it. The Student Street under the terrace, totally public and riddled with skylights, is the modern manifestation of the infinite corridor. The street winds around and through the buildings connecting the public elements of the program into the campus community.

The academic clients in the Center will be well served, too. Their neighborhoods within the Dreyfoos and Gates Buildings are creatively designed to foster locally secure neighborhoods, while the fourth-floor plaza, where meeting rooms, lounge areas, and food and beverage services are collected, constitutes a small academic village. The quality and variety of the community and public spaces will drive the success of the Stata Center. Just as at two other Gehry projects—the Guggenheim Museum in Bilbao, Spain, and the Disney Concert Hall in Los Angeles—the public interior spaces of the Stata Center have a simple, inspiring grandness about them that each day will be a joy to the people who reside there.

Finally the Stata Center's exterior is remarkable. The elements of the buildings break the scale of the enormous 400,000-square-foot above-ground area (over six million cubic feet in volume!) and suggest the individuality of the programs and peoples that live inside. It presents to MIT's neighbors a different institution from the classical formality of the Welles Bosworth buildings along the Charles River. What is remarkable is that the same MIT that holds commencement on the grand Killian Court surrounded by the Bosworth buildings can change our identity to embrace Frank Gehry's new vision of space for our academic community and its place in Cambridge and the world. Some will call the design eclectic. I think of it as a sign of the continual evolution and leadership of MIT.

—Robert A. Brown

Acknowledgments

This book, like other books of its kind, is the creation of many people.

First, I would like to thank Bob Brown who believed in the importance of documenting the design and construction process of the Stata Center. Without his enthusiasm and financial backing, *Building Stata* would never have gotten off the ground.

Since the very first discussions about the book, Chris Terman, the client representative and a gifted computer scientist in his own right, has been my sounding board, collaborating on the conceptual content and offering me private space to work when I needed it. He is also responsible for the book's introduction, a labor of love from a man who has been a part of the MIT culture for thirty years.

Early in the project, John Guttag, head of the Electrical Engineering and Computer Science Department, had the presence of mind to send me the perfect photographer, some-

one who had never photographed a construction site. Richard Sobol has been living this project with me from almost the beginning. His outsider's view and incredible eye for the human dimension has resulted in a remarkable set of photographs, which are evidence of the skills and commitment of the construction team and a key component of the Stata story. Vivid in color and composition, awesome in depth and detail, Richard's photos sometimes cause me to catch my breath. Richard has also interviewed many of the workers on site, bringing an additional dimension to the story of the building of Stata.

Having sat in weekly work sessions with Chris, Richard, and Brian Hotchkiss and Peter Blaiwas from Vern Associates, it is hard to see this book as anything but a collaborative effort. Peter's graphic sensibilities brought the many divergent materials into a cohesive whole. Brian's editing crafted technical jar-

gon into clear language understood by practitioners and laypeople alike. As a group we charted the direction of the story through iterative discussions. The course of the book truly evolved, growing from the concept of a picture book into one that provides rich and varied information about MIT as well as the design and construction of the Stata Center.

I'd like to thank Frank Urbanowski, former director of the MIT Press, Larry Cohen, the Press's former editor in chief, and Ann Wolpert, director of MIT Libraries, for their initial interest and encouragement. To Ellen Faran, director of MIT Press, and Terry Lamoureux, production manager, and all their staff, thank you for introducing me to the intricacies of the publishing process. I have a real appreciation for what you do.

President Charles Vest, Provost Robert Brown, and former Dean of Architecture William Mitchell took the time to contribute their unique

perspectives on the project. Their contribution is a testament to the importance of this new building to the Institute.

John Curry, Vicky Sirianni, and Paul Curley continually supported and encouraged me to produce this book, even in the midst of an aggressive building schedule.

Frank Gehry graciously agreed to contribute his commentary on the process and the creative underpinnings of his design. Much of the material for the commentary was a result of a walk with Frank through the building.

I appreciate all the people who contributed to the content through their review, comments, and the use of their words and images—Steve Benz, Frances Bonet, Mike Dempsey, Ellen Hanley, Paul Hewins, Robb Hewitt, Chris Kelley, John Kibiloski, Thomas Kim, Sarah Kirshner, Wilfried Kramb, Dave Lewis, Alex Martin, Keith McPeters, Keith Mendenhall, Tony Montiero, Jenny

O'Neill, Marc Salette, Wallace Floyd Associates, James Wrisley, and Bill Zahner. Your contributions added clarity and precision to the text.

To my colleagues on the Stata Project Management Team—Bob Cunkelman, François Exilhomme Dave Lewis, Rob McDevitt, Tony Montiero, Sudy Nally, David Silverman, and Susan Skrupa—thank you for your continued interest and support.

And finally, I would like to thank my husband, Fred Gould, for his ongoing support, and my daughter, McKenzie, who helped organize early material for the book.

—Nancy E. Joyce

At the start of excavation, in January 2001, I made my first visit to the Stata Center construction site and was given a tour by the safety superintendent. As he pointed out some of the hazards and dangers of the process around me, he used words such as maim, cripple, and pulverize to enlighten me on the power of heavy machines. Together we established a protocol that allowed me unlimited access to the site providing that an escort shadowed me as I worked. Although I was used to working alone, I was grateful to know that my safety was considered more important than getting the next photograph. For their companionship, conversation,

shouts of warning, and occasional life-saving shoves, I am indebted to Keith Brown, François Exilhomme, McKenzie Gould, Rob McDevitt, Mike Pino, Susan Skrupa, Chris Terman, and James Wrisley.

The Skanska USA Building site superintendents were always willing to answer my construction questions, point me to a newly exposed vantage point, and show me where the ladders were when I was stranded on a fresh slab of concrete. My thanks to Jerry Albert, Ed Dubois, Paul Hewins, Chris Kelley, Claude LeBlanc, Scott MacKenzie, Adam Maxcy, Neil Webster, and Bill Young.

—Richard M. Sobol

Dedication

The Stata Center will be blessed for years to come with the quality workmanship left behind by the men and women who contributed their best. This book is dedicated to them and especially to Marc Salette and Paul Hewins, whose individual integrity and mutual respect set the standard for all others to follow.

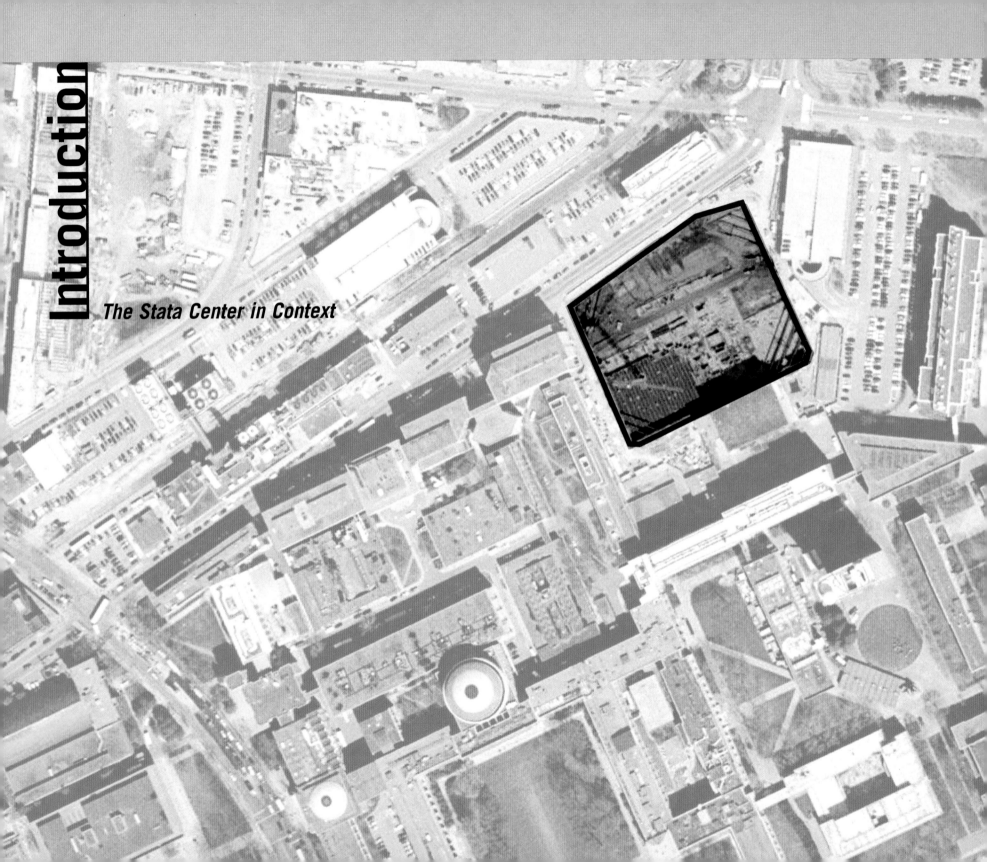

Introduction

The Stata Center in Context

Intertwined Destinies: The Charles River and MIT

In 1776 Cambridge was a small, fortified hamlet on the north side of the Charles River estuary. The red diamond in the tidal flats indicates the Stata Center's eventual site.

Admittedly, Frank Gehry's Ray and Maria Stata Center is quite a departure from the buildings that constitute the Massachusetts Institute of Technology campus. To understand how that happened, it is worthwhile to look at just how the surroundings came to be the way they are and why things have come out differently this time.

Colonial Boston was built on a peninsula bounded to the north and west by a shallow tidal estuary with its surrounding salt marshes, which became mud flats at low tide, and to the east and south by the city's harbor. The tight confines of Boston proper led to the development of active communities across the harbor, but even with the establishment of Harvard College in 1636, colonial Cambridge remained a small, rather separate community, reached from Boston either by ferry from Charlestown or by a circuitous eight-mile overland journey via Roxbury and Muddy River Village (known today—more elegantly—as Brookline).

In 1793, the travel distance from Boston to Cambridge was reduced to three miles with the construction of the West Boston Bridge, predecessor to the current Longfellow Bridge. The mercantile and industrial districts of Cambridgeport and East Cambridge sprang up along the roads leading from the bridge to the Cambridge Common. Over time, these settlements expanded,

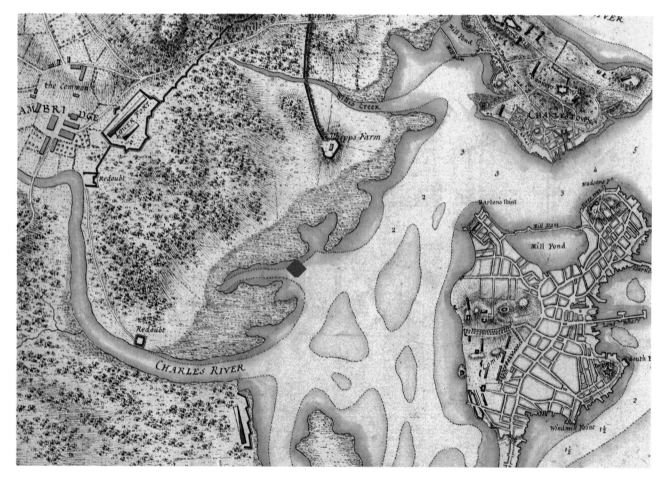

merged, and finally incorporated as the City of Cambridge in 1846.

Meanwhile, similar industrial developments were being established on the Boston side of the estuary. The Roxbury Mill Dam, constructed in 1821 along what is now Beacon Street, housed a tide-powered mill. Unfortunately, the dam slowed the daily tidal action that had effectively removed the ever-increasing quantities of city sewage flowing into Back Bay. In 1835, construction of causeways for the Worcester and Providence railroads further exacerbated the problem and, according to the contemporary press, Back Bay degenerated into "the foulest marsh and muddy flats to be found anywhere in Massachusetts."

Boston responded in 1837 by filling the portion of the bay adjacent to the Boston Common to create the Public Garden. But the lagoon continued to fester, and in 1857 the legislature finally acted, reclaiming title to the flats, purchasing gravel landfill from Needham, and commencing a twenty-five-year project to fill in Back Bay.

In 1859 the governor proposed

that some of this newly created land be used for the purpose of education. William Barton Rogers actively pursued this opportunity, arguing that the creation of a school of

industrial science "would be largely conducive to the progress of the industrial arts and sciences throughout the Commonwealth." His goal for the school was to transcend the

This 1878 harbor map shows a thriving industrial Cambridge and the reclamation of Back Bay. The three black dots located between the S and T in BOSTON are MIT's original buildings at Copley Square.

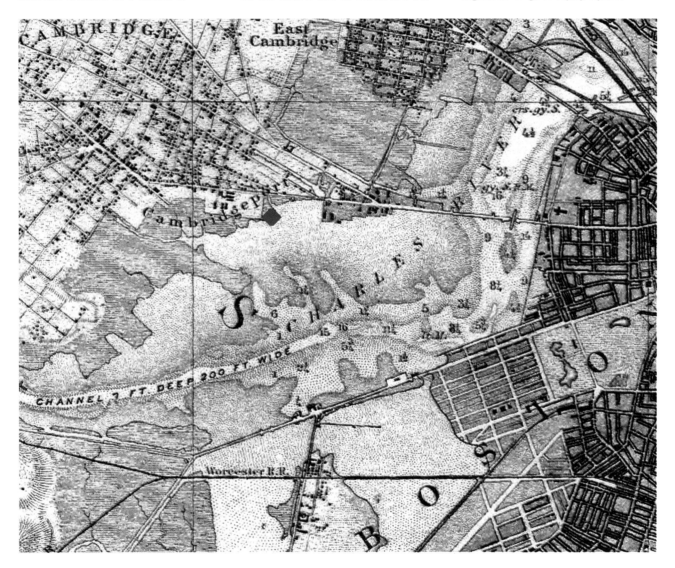

facing page:
Judging from the number of lots shown on this 1900 insurance map, the developers hoped that another Back Bay would develop on the Cambridge side of the Charles River.

tradition of rote learning of engineering concepts by stimulating investigation of the scientific principles underlying industrial applications. In 1861, Rogers's third petition was favorably received by the legislature, which granted a block of newly created land in Back Bay, one third of it for a museum of natural history and two thirds for the Massachusetts Institute of Technology. Classes began on February 20, 1865, with an enrollment of fifteen students. Over the next forty years the Institute slowly expanded its campus in the vicinity of Copley Square.

The notion of creating urban land was clearly too good an idea to use only once—and in 1881 a group of developers incorporated the Charles River Embankment Company. Not having easy access to the Needham gravel deposits, Cambridge filled its side of the estuary with soil from the excavations for the Boston subway and mud dredged from the bottom of the estuary to create the Charles River basin. In 1887 the Commonwealth approved the construction of a bridge from

Boston's West Chester Park to Massachusetts Avenue in Cambridge. In the autumn of 1891, the newly christened Harvard Bridge was opened to the public.

Much of Cambridge's newly created land lay south of Albany Street and the adjacent railroad. The academically inspired Cambridge investors optimistically laid out a series of streets with names such as Vassar, Wellesley, Princeton, and Amherst. But development was slow to take hold, and by 1900 the only significant buildings were located along Massachusetts Avenue: the massive Metropolitan Storage Warehouse, by the railroad, and the

River Bank Court Apartments at the foot of the Harvard Bridge.

Though MIT rapidly established credentials as an innovator in technology and education, its existence as an independent entity was by no means ensured during the second half of the nineteenth century. Tough economic times played havoc with the Institute's finances. More significant, however, were pressures to consider a union with Harvard. Charles Eliot, who developed a considerable reputation as an educator while on the MIT faculty, was appointed president of Harvard in 1869. Just a few months into his tenure he proposed merging MIT with Harvard's ailing Lawrence Scientific School. The members of the MIT Corporation voted down this and several subsequent merger proposals.

In 1904, flush with a recent large bequest for applied science, Eliot proposed for a final time that MIT move from its Back Bay home and become Harvard's engineering school. A group headed by Andrew Carnegie purchased land—where the Harvard Business School now stands—in anticipation of the merger. This time, faced with a shortage of resources, the MIT Corporation voted in favor of the merger, overriding the faculty and alumni, who had by an overwhelming majority voted to remain independent. But the merger hinged on selling the Institute's Copley Square properties in order to fund the new campus buildings and in a subsequent ruling, the Supreme Judicial Court denied MIT clear title to the properties, thus preventing the sale and derailing the merger.

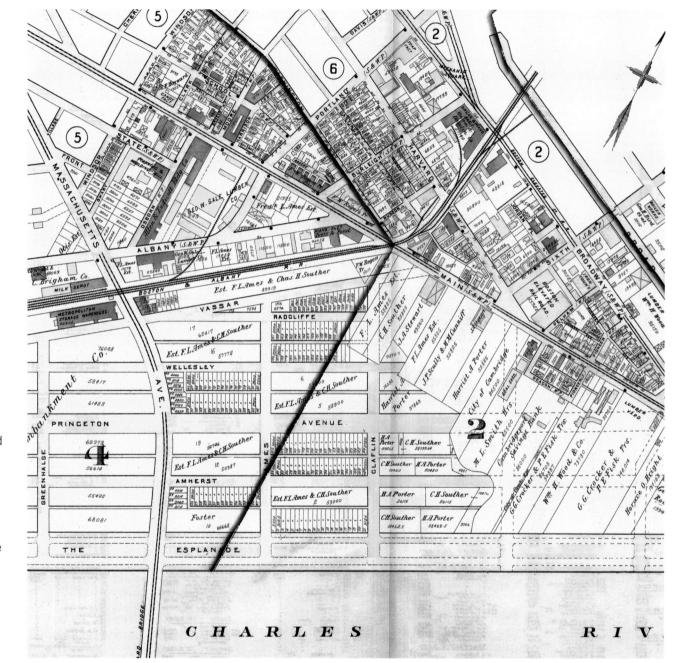

Campus Beginnings

In 1909, Richard C. Maclaurin became MIT's president and immediately started the search for a new campus. According to the 1916 campus-dedication program, "it was recognized by everyone that the time had come for a change. The buildings at Copley Square were outworn, crowded, inconvenient; it was neither possible nor desirable to multiply them around the old site in the heart of the city. There must be a place not only for greater shops and laboratories, but for dormitories for the homeless students from half across the world. The time had come to move."

Maclaurin had already noticed the swath of undeveloped land just across the river from MIT's Back Bay campus. Indeed, the day before his inauguration he had visited the site and later established that it was available for purchase. Other locations near and far were also considered, most notably land along Commonwealth Avenue just west of Boston University Bridge and a site offered by alumni and located in Springfield, Massachusetts.

T. Coleman du Pont (class of 1884), who had made a significant donation for the acquisition of the new campus, urged Maclaurin to think big: "Technology will occupy a great position in the future and must have room to grow," he cautioned. In 1911, Maclaurin announced that for the sum of $775,000, the Institute had acquired 46 acres for a new campus on the Cambridge banks of the Charles River.

In *When MIT Was "Boston Tech,"* *1861–1916*, Samuel Prescott relates how Maclaurin raised the construction funds: Frank W. Lovejoy (class of 1894), general manager of Eastman Kodak Company, wrote that George Eastman, the company's president, "would be inclined to help out." Maclaurin arranged to meet Eastman in New York and described MIT's potential. When Eastman was about to leave, he suddenly asked, "What will it cost to put up the new buildings?"

"About two and a half million dollars," Maclaurin replied. "I'll send you a draft," was Eastman's response. At his request, Eastman's gift remained anonymous, sparking much speculation over the identity of the "mysterious Mr. Smith" before the secret was revealed in 1920.

But financial issues delayed the start of construction: once again, legal difficulties complicated the sale of the downtown campus, which was needed to raise construction funds. (In the end, the Institute kept the old Rogers Building until 1938, to house the Department of Architecture.) The design was scrutinized for possible economies, such as using brick instead of limestone for the facade and eliminating the main dome and the circular auditorium underneath. Happily for the current residents of campus, the architect prevailed, and both the limestone and dome were kept (the decision makers justified retaining the latter feature by using it to house the library). But despite Maclaurin's careful supervision, the cost of the building grew, and eventually he reported to Mr. Eastman that his gift would not cover the expected costs. Prescott reported that "so tactfully was the information phrased that Mr. Eastman, who was already certain that no waste had been permitted, made a further contribution of $500,000, with the implied promise of an additional gift if and when it should prove necessary."

The first concrete was poured in 1913, and by 1916 the new campus was ready for use. The new buildings provided about one million square feet of teaching, research, and dormitory space serving 1,900 students and 300 teaching staff at a cost of just under $7 million. Construction required 25,000 piles to stabilize the landfill, five million bricks, and 465 carloads of Indiana limestone.

Choosing to relocate from a residential area in Back Bay to an industrial district in Cambridge worked out well in subsequent years. The City of Cambridge has generally welcomed the reclamation of declining industrial sites to establish more sustainable educational activities, and the campus now encompasses more than 150 acres. Perhaps more important, potential battles between an expanding campus and adjacent residential neighborhoods—a perennial thorn in Harvard's side—have been avoided.

William Welles Bosworth's rendering of the new campus as seen from the Charles River. The fifty-foot-tall statue of Minerva in the main court did not survive the budget crunch.

Campus Architecture and the Infinite Corridor

The search for an appropriate design for the new campus also involved considerable exploration of alternatives. Plans from numerous other universities were consulted, and the latest techniques for construction, lighting, and ventilation were investigated. Hoping to be chosen as architect, John R. Freeman (class of 1876) used his own funds to study what sort of campus might be built on the Cambridge side of the Charles River. He proposed "architectural details and outlines derived from the Greek Classic style, which have satisfied the human eye for 2,000 years" and a unified building "avoiding to the maximum extent the need for men racing across lots, often scantily clad, from one building to another in Boston's raw climate."

Freeman was "strongly of the opinion that college architects spent too much time on exteriors, designing monuments rather than functional buildings." He laid out his own vision for the new campus in Study No. 7, articulating his "belief that the problem must be worked out from the inside. First of all, we must obtain a flood of <u>window light</u>; Second, a flood of <u>fresh air</u> under perfect control; Third, an <u>efficiency</u> and avoidance of lost motion by student and teacher, equal to that which obtains in our best industrial works. And Fourth, the consideration of the psychology of student life, the cultivation of the social instincts, the development of <u>personal contact</u>, must strongly control the layout of the very masonry." Interestingly, Freeman's goals (underscored above) parallel the charge given to the architect for the Stata Center.

In 1912, William Welles Bosworth (class of 1889) was chosen as the architect and Stone and Webster Engineering Corporation was given responsibility for actual construction. Many of Freeman's ideas found their way into Bosworth's design although the final layout of the academic buildings, with a central great court and a Pantheon-like dome, owes much to Thomas Jefferson's University of Virginia. The campus plan called for locating the academic buildings at the west side of campus, along

Massachusetts Avenue, with the residential buildings and athletic fields occupying the east side.

Bosworth's floor plans for the original "Main Group" of academic buildings reflected the influence of the efficient, functional industrial architecture of the time. The basic building block was a thirty- or thirty-two-foot bay; the exact measure was dictated by the maximum practical column spacing afforded by reinforced-concrete construction. This block was organized along either side of a central eight-foot-wide corridor, which was repeated for whatever length and on as many floors as desirable. The bays were easily divided into labs and offices but could also be left undivided, creating large, multistory spaces to

accommodate machinery. These long, relatively narrow "bar buildings" have proved very adaptable, allowing for hundreds of alterations over the years. Indeed, much subsequent construction has followed the template established by the original Main Group. As Eero Saarinen observed, "It seems to me that for academic instruction, space such as that in the old MIT buildings provides an excellent example of what in the long run proves to be economical space."

The interconnected central corridors are collectively known as the "infinite corridor." (When capitalized, the name refers to a particular 762-foot-long corridor that serves as the main spine of campus, running east-west through buildings 8, 4,

facing page:
This 1928 aerial photo shows the Main Group on the west (left) side of campus with the dorms, commons, and athletic fields to the east.

For many years, multistory machinery spaces (inset) provided hands-on engineering experience for students.

The Compton Lab (Building 26) is a classic bar building (below). The plan at left shows how a public corridor is sandwiched between offices on one side and labs on the other.

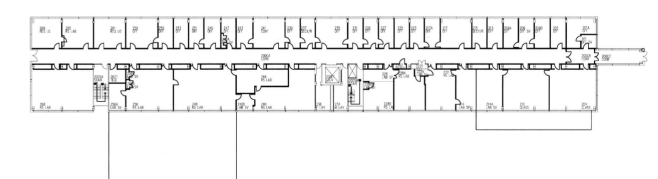

A segment of MIT's (in)famous infinite corridor.

10, 3, and 7, respectively.) The infinite corridor has become a symbol of both the good and not-so-good aspects of MIT culture. On the good side, it has played host to innumerable chance encounters that have led to productive, albeit unplanned, conversations—a physical embodiment of how the scientific and engineering disciplines are interconnected. On the not-so-good side, however, the infinite corridor can seem anonymous and impersonal. As the MIT community has grown to more than 10,000 students, 950 faculty, and 8,400 other employees, the sheer number of people passing through can be daunting. Since the infinite corridor runs past every office, doors that once might have been open to welcome colleagues are now closed to ward off interruptions from strangers. Rather than bringing people together, therefore, the corridor often promotes insularity. This is unfortunate for researchers, especially those with a predilection for a heads-down, monastic-style existence.

The Building 20 Era

During the 1920s and 1930s, MIT continued on the path charted first by Rogers and then Maclaurin: attracting a faculty actively engaged in scientific and engineering investigations, as well as bright and ambitious students from around the world. The campus grew at a modest but steady rate, adding to the Main Group according to the plan envisioned by Bosworth: academic buildings for specific disciplines, such as the Pratt School of Naval Architecture (Building 5, 1920), the Guggenheim Aeronautical Laboratory (Building 33, 1928), the Eastman Laboratories for chemistry and physics (Building 6, 1933), and the Rogers Building, housing the School of Architecture (Building 7, 1938).

Expediency did lead to one major change in the overall campus plan. As the country emerged from the Great Depression and enrollments were once again on the rise, a desperate need arose for campus housing beyond what could be supplied by the East Campus dormitories. Commercial residential buildings along the river to the west of Massachusetts Avenue offered a ready-made solution and in 1937 the Institute purchased the Riverbank Court Hotel (now Ashdown House) for use as a graduate student residence. Subsequent development of the residential program furthered the growth of a "west campus" along the river, taking advantage of the pleasant prospect. The abundant open space behind the buildings provided a fine location for athletic fields.

World War II had a profound impact on the role MIT was to play in the advancement of science and technology. The Institute's alumni and faculty firmly believed in the fundamental importance of scientific investigation as the basis for technological development. They were among those who took the lead in articulating a wartime mission for the scientific and engineering community, establishing extraordinarily productive multi-disciplinary labs.

MIT was home to many such labs; the best known included the Radiation Laboratory (the RadLab) and the Servomechanism Lab (the ServoLab). The RadLab was charged with developing the British-invented resonant cavity magnetron into a detection system that would bounce ten-centimeter microwaves off distant objects using the returning echoes to reveal an object's position. The resulting system is more popularly known as radar. The

4,000-member RadLab staff (among such wartime groups it was second in size only to the staff of the Manhattan Project) designed more than 150 different systems over five years; four of its physicists

went on to receive Nobel Prizes for later work. The ServoLab, working closely with MIT aeronautics professor Charles "Doc" Draper, developed weapons-control systems based on Doc's gyroscopic gun sight—the

Building 20, home of the RadLab, seen from the Vassar Street facade. Note the platform for the radar apparatus on the roof.

precessing of the gyros was used to calculate the correct aiming point for fast-moving aerial targets.

The RadLab was housed in part in a complex of timber-framed buildings rapidly assembled in the Northeast Sector of campus. Arranged as classic bar buildings, in later years they possessed a certain dilapidated charm—with unpretentious exteriors and eminently modifiable interiors. Several were put to other uses after the war: Building 22 was converted into housing for 600 students until the mid-1950s. Building 20 continued to house departmental offices, labs, shops, teaching spaces, and model railroads (!) until it was demolished in 1999 to make way for the Stata Center. Its residents happily christened it the Magical Incubator in honor of the many productive activities, both official and unofficial, that it had sheltered over the decades.

The problem-solving atmosphere in the wartime labs—geared toward rapid development in a flexible, nonbureaucratic environment—produced remarkable results,

changing the course of the war. It also changed the world's expectations of science and technology: in 1945 MIT president Karl Compton wrote, "In these five years the Institute spent on its war contracts as much money [$117 million] as it had spent on its normal activities during its previous 80 years of existence. This is a sobering thought; it makes one wonder what tremendous things could be accomplished in peacetime if the same energy, determination, and resources were marshaled to fashion a better world." These expectations were to fuel a tremendous growth in the Institute over the succeeding half-century.

One important type of "fuel" is the money needed to fund all aspects of Institute life: operating expenses, maintenance of the physical plant, salaries and benefits for faculty and staff, administrative overheads, stipends for teaching and research assistants, capital expenditures, student aid, and so on. Philanthropy, including endowment income, has always been the major source of operating funds for the Institute. During the war,

however, MIT vice president (later president) James Killian and others negotiated with the government to perform research and development at cost, an amount that included direct expenses—salaries, benefits, equipment, travel—and an agreed-upon allowance for indirect costs—space, utilities, administration.

Thus the wartime and postwar boom in government-funded research both permitted an expansion of the Institute's faculty and staff and financed the construction of new academic buildings. Both of these advances took place at a rate substantially greater than what would have been possible based on philanthropy alone. Having both the need and the wherewithal, MIT grew by leaps and bounds: in the twenty-five years between its move to Cambridge and World War II, the Institute had added only nineteen buildings, doubling the available space to 2 million square feet. In the twenty-five years since World War II, the Institute added forty-one buildings, providing an additional 3.6 million square feet of space.

"High Tech" and the Northeast Sector

By the mid-1970s MIT had largely completed the build-out of the main campus—the area between Massachusetts Avenue and Ames Street—leaving only the Northeast Sector to be developed.

For the first twenty-five years, this corner of campus had been something of a backdoor, as it bordered on an active industrial area in what then was the second-largest industrial city in Massachusetts. Plants near campus manufactured diverse products such as boilers, carbon paper, candy, fasteners, pickles, and typewriter ribbons. After World War II, however, much of this activity was relocated elsewhere, leaving behind a large inventory of antiquated and obsolete buildings.

The area north and east of campus languished until the mid-1960s, when the construction of Technology Square (home to Polaroid Corporation's headquarters) and the selection of Kendall Square as the site of the $64 million NASA Electronics Research Center sparked a round of redevelopment. This effort faltered when NASA pulled out just after the 1969 landing on the moon, but it revived again in 1975 when the government approved $6 million in Section 112 credits to fund projects located within a certain distance of the MIT campus. These monies launched the construction of the massive Cambridge Center office and retail complex. Happily, another piece of the puzzle fell into place at the same time because the nascent "high-tech" industry demanded more work space.

Computers played an increasingly important role in science and engineering during the 1960s and 1970s. At that time, these expensive, room-size pieces of equipment were often shared by large

The light industrial area north of MIT's main campus circa 1950 with the Mason & Hamlin Piano Factory in the foreground (left).

In the early 1960s, research and development functions started to replace light industry in the neighborhoods surrounding MIT (below). Since 1963, this Technology Square building has been home to MIT's computer science laboratories, which are now the primary tenants of the Stata Center.

In 1963 this IBM mainframe provided 0.35 MIPS with 128KB of memory at a cost of $3.5 million. Forty years later the student's laptop supplies 2,000 MIPS and 1GB memory at a cost of $1,500.

communities of users. However, rapid advances in the manufacture and packaging of computer circuits and memory, and the use of increasingly integrated circuits shrank computers first to desk size and then, in the early 1980s, to a box that could comfortably fit on a desktop. The advent of affordable personal computers had a dramatic effect on the workplace and led to a huge demand for modestly priced peripherals, networks to connect the

computers, and software to make it all work. The high-tech industry was off and running.

The world of high tech affected MIT in many ways. Readily available high-performance computing changed the nature of work for many engineers. Information technology streamlined research and development as staff made use of computer-based simulation and the World Wide Web. Even when using traditional experimental apparatus, researchers employed computers to sequence and control operations as well as to collect and analyze the resulting data. Many researchers now worked solely at their desks. Thus they needed work space quite different from the equipment-centered labs of the "old" MIT.

In keeping with MIT's mission, the high-tech revolution spurred new research and educational programs, this time in the areas of computer science, materials, and devices. Electrical engineering, already the largest department at MIT since 1921, expanded further to accommodate 1,100 undergraduate majors and 750 graduate

students as interest in these fields grew. The Computer Science and Artificial Intelligence Laboratory, until now housed in leased space off campus, is MIT's largest research lab, involving over 800 faculty, staff, and students. Finally, the remarkable rise in stock values, driven in large part by technology-related companies, created additional endowment income. Coupled with the philanthropy of a new generation of high-tech entrepreneurs and cost recovery from a burgeoning research program, additional funds to invest in new campus activities and space became available.

Once again, MIT was blessed with the means, motive, and opportunity to make a major addition to campus. The particular challenges were laid out in the charter for the Ray and Maria Stata Center:

- Bring MIT's computer, information, and intelligence-science researchers together under one roof on the main campus, benefiting both the researchers themselves and their colleagues in related disciplines. The building will house over 10 percent of the

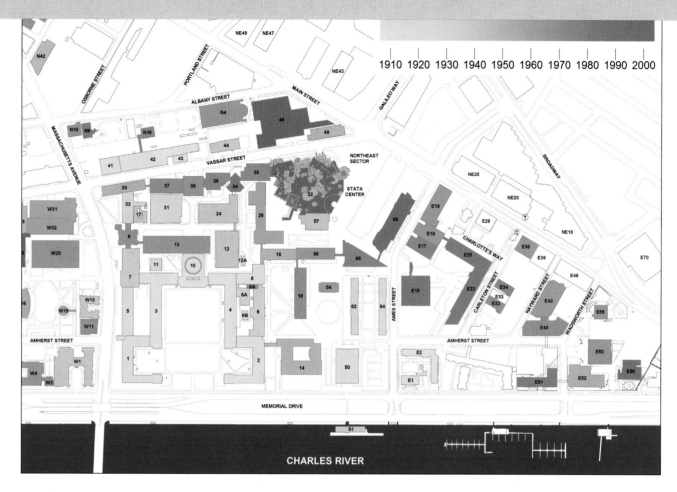

MIT faculty as well as teaching, fitness, child-care, parking, and student-life facilities.

- Create spaces designed to improve the productivity of humans rather than efficiently house apparatus—build a "people building" instead of an "equipment building."
- Consider how best to provide a gateway to the revived R&D dis-trict and transportation hub to the north and east of campus, creating a distinctive icon for MIT in the twenty-first century.

To quote Charles Vest, MIT's current president, "It is a time for substantial experimentation and calculated risks that will help us sort out opportunities and find effective paths." While MIT has many traditions, the most enduring one is the fostering of creative revolutions by thinking outside of the box. This spirit drove the design of the Stata Center.

—Christopher J. Terman

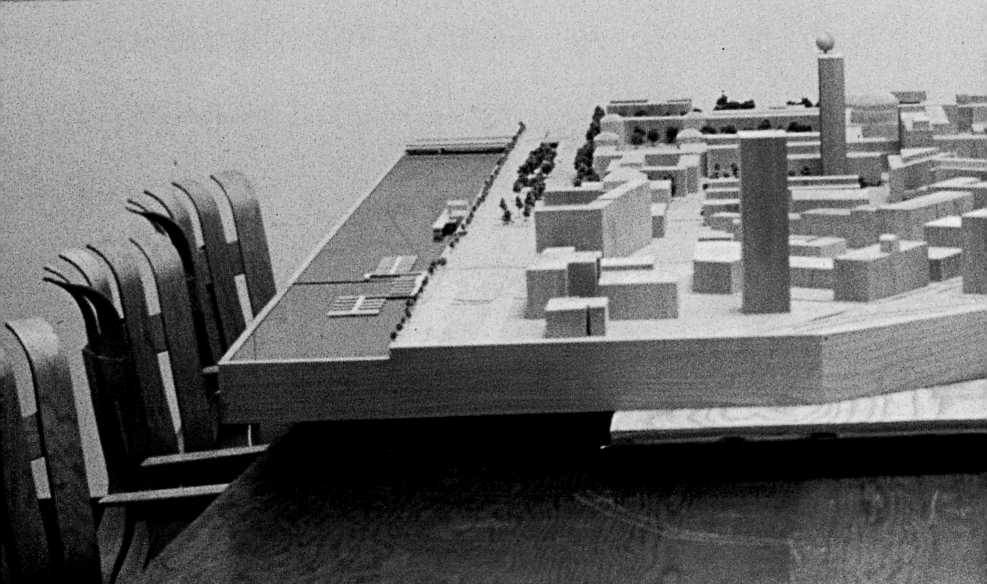

The Site

In 1989, the Northeast Sector (highlighted on this campus map) presented the last opportunity for development on MIT's main campus. Building 20, the East Garage, and an old factory building site were ready to be replaced by new academic buildings.

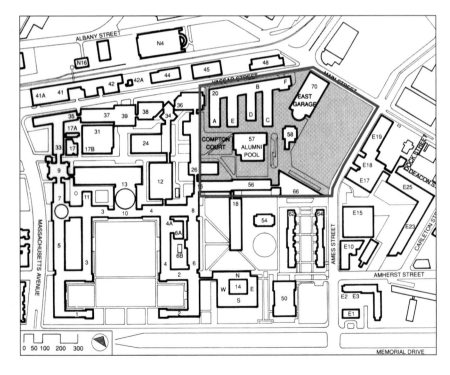

In his campus-planning study of the early twentieth century, the architect William Welles Bosworth reserved the Northeast Sector— approximately one quarter of the land originally purchased by MIT— for athletics buildings and fields. In subsequent years, however, the Institute purchased land west of the original forty acres, across Massachusetts Avenue, and began to shift the athletic functions to this area. From 1941 to 1946, the Northeast Sector was used for wartime outdoor training exercises and for research and development of war-related innovations, such as radar. With the facilities to support the war effort covering what had been playing fields, all outdoor athletic activities in this sector were relocated, leaving the Alumni Pool building as the only vestige of Bosworth's original plan for athletics.

From 1946 to 1989, all building activity on the sector took place on its perimeter. The construction of Buildings 16, 26, 56, and 66 defined the Northeast Sector as academic in character; the building mass gave architectural definition to two sides of the site. In fact, as early as 1960 the Northeast Sector was heralded for providing a new front door to the campus in a newly energized area of the City of Cambridge, where, farther to the northeast of campus, former industrial sites were being commercially developed. In 1986, one such building on the corner of the Northeast Sector became available for purchase, its demolition clearing the way for construction of the new Biology Building (Building 68). Purchase of the additional land and the impending demolition of Building 20 provided impetus for a new planning study to ensure that the Biology Building and subsequent development on the sector would make the best possible use of the land.

With this 1989 study, conducted by Wallace Floyd and Associates, the story of the Ray and Maria Stata Center begins. This document guided the design team as it addressed issues such as circulation, open space, services, and utilities. It also outlined allotment of square footage for other buildings proposed for the sector. The planning objectives for these buildings were stated briefly: "Buildings will contain spaces that foster fruitful interactions, be connected by inside and outside paths, and have flexibility to accommodate a variety of uses for the future, and open spaces will be hospitable and inviting."

The study comprised two parts: the first stated the underlying criteria just summarized; the other recommended ways to implement those criteria. This second part proposed the massing of the new buildings and a layout of the footprints. The massing was based on zoning criteria of the time as well as MIT's stated desire that the width of new buildings range from sixty-eight to seventy-two feet, which was generally considered an efficient, flexible size for a science building at that time. The site layout also massed the buildings at the exterior of the site, allowing for maximum campus space inside.

The construction of the Biology Building generally followed the criteria set out by this study as well as recommendations for its massing and layout. But nine years later, when funding was available to build a new center for intelligence sciences, the proposed new building exceeded the size assumptions of the 1989 study. In addition, the

Building 20, constructed during World War II as a temporary building to develop radar, still functioned as research space until its demolition in 1998. Sited at the edge of the original land that MIT purchased for its Cambridge campus, it bordered an old industrial section of the City of Cambridge.

latest thinking concerning development of science buildings was starting to challenge the sixty-eight-to-seventy-two-foot bar-building concept. To ensure that 1989 criteria could still be achieved and that their concept was still sound, the Institute decided to include a master-planning study in the scope of the work undertaken by the architect of the new center. This study would review, challenge, and build upon Wallace Floyd's recommendations and criteria.

The new building was intended to house groups of researchers: computer and communication scientists, and researchers in linguistics and philosophy. For thirty-five years, most of them had been working off campus in rented space. Clearing Building 20 from the Northeast Sector created the opportunity to bring them together in a complex of buildings on the main part of campus.

Once the Institute secured funding, through a generous gift from Ray and Maria Stata, a request for

This plan and model from the Wallace Floyd 1989 planning study show how a full build-out of the Northeast Sector envisioned long, rectangular buildings that continued the traditional massing of the other main-campus buildings. The proposed buildings would complete the perimeter established by existing buildings along Vassar and Ames Streets, thus creating a sequence of interior courtyards.

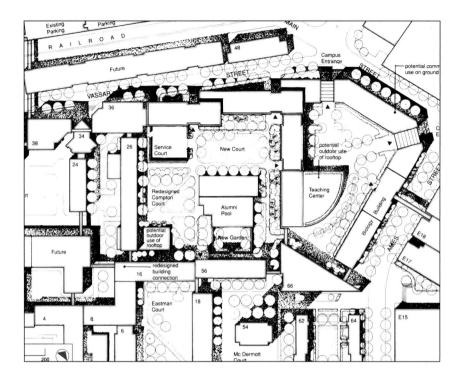

proposal was sent out to sixteen firms, chosen by a committee that included the dean of architecture, the director of facilities, and a researcher, who was elected by his colleagues to represent them. The choice was narrowed to five firms; each was invited for a separate all-day interview. Out of this process, MIT hired the firm of Frank O. Gehry and Associates, based in Santa Monica, California.

One of Frank Gehry's strengths, evident both in the interview and in MIT's subsequent research on his firm's work, is his ability to see a project in its overall context. That strength, coupled with his unusual design process, convinced the Institute that he was a good match for this project. Combining analysis of existing site conditions, discussions with the Institute, development of many site models, and review of the criteria established in the Wallace Floyd plan, Frank Gehry studied the site while he established some conceptual ideas for the building itself. The firm issued a report in 1998 that validated the criteria established in 1989 but suggested a very different method of implementing them.

One of the most visible differences in implementation is in the massing of the buildings on the site. According to the 1989 proposal, the buildings would hug the exterior of the site to maximize open space for the campus. Gehry's design opened the campus to the city, stepping the building back from Vassar Street and breaking up the building mass. In addition, Gehry's plan challenged the concept of the bar building, with its rigid dimensions. The researcher's requirements called for windows that optimized natural light and airflow, and Gehry felt this could be achieved better through other geometries. The Gehry plan also excluded vehicles from the Northeast Sector by putting the shipping and receiving service underground and directly accessible from Vassar Street, a public way.

During the course of design, other opportunities further challenged the 1989 implementation plan. The building footprint moved toward the Alumni pool, encompass-ing it as part of the new composition. Also, the underground service facility freed up space on the ground level, which now could be used for student functions. Interestingly, although the implementation is very different from that envisioned by Wallace Floyd, the criteria underlying all Gehry's subsequent moves—flexibility, connectivity, collaborative work spaces, and inviting outdoor spaces—are very much in the same spirit.

The Program

As part of their study, Gehry's firm also incorporated specific goals set forth by the Stata Center's prospective users—researchers in intelligence sciences, primarily computer scientists. Frank Gehry's interaction with them and the nature of research at MIT itself inspired the development of both the master plan and the building program.

The researchers had heretofore worked in fields that shared many similar goals, especially at the overlapping edges of their research. But the Laboratory for Computer Science (LCS), Artificial Intelligence (AI), the Laboratory for Information Decisions Systems (LIDS), and the Linguistics and Philosophy Department (L&P)—the intended occupants of the Stata Center—were housed in different areas, both on and off campus. MIT's hope is that the right type of physical environ-ment will foster interactions around those overlapping edges that will result in the creation of whole new research explorations.

Throughout the twentieth century, MIT's infinite corridor of interconnected buildings has been credited as a component of the physical infrastructure that enhances collaboration—it both symbolically and physically blurs lines among academic departments.

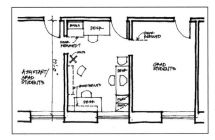

In his conversations with the researchers who would occupy new offices in the Stata Center, Frank Gehry noted that the more they described what they wanted in their new spaces, the more they described their present spaces, like those shown in this photograph and plan. His challenge was to get researchers to envision their work lives differently.

This infrastructure has created a culture of research-focused groupings rather than the discrete academic departments that prevail on many campuses. The Ray and Maria Stata Center carries on this tradition by being organized as research neighborhoods; by being linked to adjacent buildings; by creating places where collaboration can happen casually and easily; and by building a home for work that can be altered readily in response to new initiatives.

In his speech announcing the generous gift by Ray and Maria Stata, MIT's president, Charles Vest, laid out a charter for the occupants of the building:

"As we approach the end of the twentieth century and the advent of the twenty-first, information technol-ogy has become ubiquitous, complex, yet increasingly accessible. Its rate of technological advance remains astounding. Great challenges and opportunities abound as we seek to make modern information technology serve humankind by enhancing the quality of life, by rendering boundaries of time and space meaningless, and by improving human understanding. New architectures, new ways of integrating technologies, new information marketplaces, and new unifying principles must be developed. MIT's researchers will continue to lead the way in this important mission, doing so in a creative environment that integrates world-class research, education, and interaction with the commercial and governmental sectors."

Before the master-planning and programming studies were begun, the MIT researchers answered President Vest's challenge by expressing their goals and expectations concerning the new building and how it would contribute to their evolving research needs. This document served as the programming guide throughout the project. Its main points are listed here:

1. Create a long-term home for the building's occupants that supports collaborative and flexible research environments and frequent social and intellectual interactions at the same time as it provides a workplace with good access to outside light and air.

2. Integrate the building's occupants into campus circulation by providing unobtrusive but effective security that allows for an open research environment, connections to research groups in adjacent buildings, access to teaching spaces, and extension of the infinite corridor. This integration must be accomplished while minimizing the impact on privacy, research, and social activities within the Center.

3. Define the essence of the research and the Institute through the architectural expression of the building, which will convey a sense of expectation and excitement and capture the researchers' vigor, boldness, and vision.

4. Incorporate new technology and optimize building performance by exploring environmentally responsible systems, products, and technical innovations. Anticipate new technologies and accommodate their eventual integration into the building.

The new Center is home to three research laboratories and one academic department. The integration of these four entities into a single complex is the overarching goal of the program. At the same time, each will maintain a strong individual sense of identity. These two goals are achieved through interconnected research groupings and shared facilities, along with clear boundaries and entrances. A teaching center on the ground floor and other community program elements constitute the public components of the Center. While unencumbered connectivity exists inside the research areas, access from the public spaces is controlled.

The heart of the building program is the research groups. These groups, typically organized around a single faculty member or principal investigator, number from ten to fifteen individuals. Funded by grants lasting from three to five years, these groups are assembled to conduct research that includes computation, theory, software, hardware, and robotics. An individual group's space must accommodate quiet work, exchange of ideas, and demonstrations made to colleagues, visitors, and grant agencies. Since members of the group share work space as well as tools, books, and materials, security is of prime importance. As research projects change, groups evolve in size, requiring that the physical boundaries be at once permeable and flexible.

While the research labs comprise most of the building program, the Stata Center also houses the Department of Linguistics and Philosophy. Unlike the research labs, which break out into small, identifiable groups, this department is essentially made up of two larger groups. In addition, the way they work and collaborate differs distinctly from that of the computer scientists;

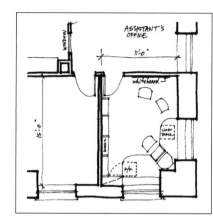

linguists and philosophers have a more individualistic style, and their collaboration involves two or three individuals rather than teams or small groups. However, the intellectual synergy between their work and that of the computer scientists makes the potential for interactions all the more exciting. To achieve this goal, the program stresses the need for common resources to which all groups in the building will be drawn.

With the computer central to the work lives of Stata Center researchers, issues such as ergonomics, heat recovery from computer power units, glare from natural light, and storage of the central processing units were considered in planning office layouts and furnishings.

Urban Design

The 1998 master-planning effort undertaken by Frank Gehry and Associates emphasized how the Northeast Sector would engage the city around it. The team considered the future development of the Main-Vassar-Galileo intersection and how it could evolve into a definitive urban and civic space, with the Institute and the City of Cambridge mutually benefiting from it. What is now an edge of campus will one day be a focal point, as the campus continues to expand northward and as the city continues to develop the areas around the sector. The mixed-use development proposed for the site directly across from the sector, the recent renovation and addition to Technology Square and its subsequent purchase by MIT, and the construction of the Brain and Cognitive Science building directly across on Vassar Street are changing the face of this part of the city. In addition, the Institute, in collaboration with the city, has redesigned Vassar Street. The new street will be pedestrian oriented, with bike paths, significant plantings, and new paving. These developments, along with the existing Whitehead Institute and the new Stata Center, require a powerful organizational device to define a sense of place. The 1998 planning study proposed a plaza at the corner of Vassar and Main Streets to organize these components and create a dynamic public space, which will also serve as a new gateway to the main campus.

The Stata Center constitutes the second phase (the Biology Building was the first) of a proposed build-out for the Northeast Sector of the main campus. Future phases anticipate the creation of the Teaching and Learning Center and the

The Stata Center is situated at the corner of Vassar (A) and Main (B) Streets, two principal pedestrian and vehicular approaches to campus. It also stands at the end of Galileo Way (C) and offers a surprising vista to the traveler rounding the bend toward Vassar Street.

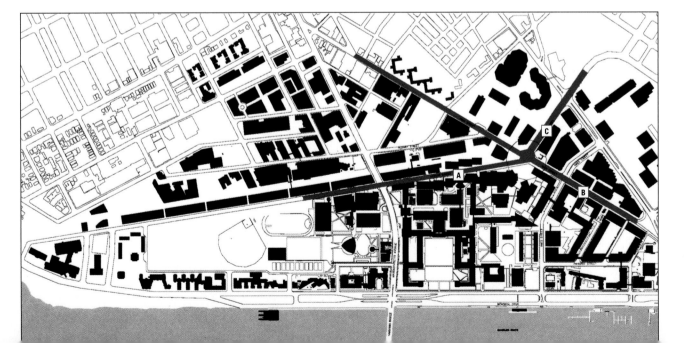

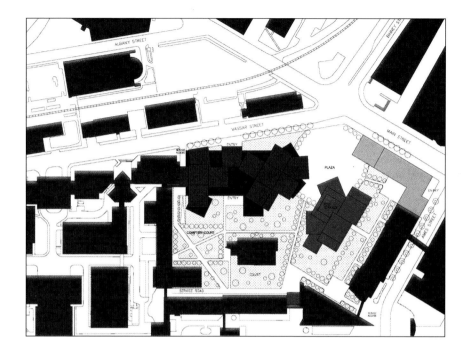

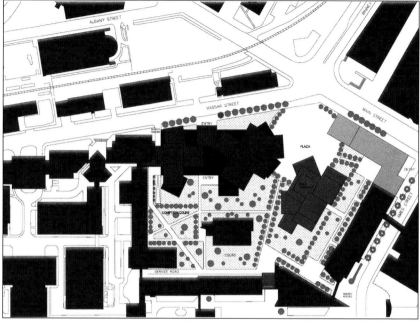

expansion of the Biology Building. With the full build-out, the Stata Center, the Biology Building extension, and the auditorium of the Teaching and Learning Center will frame the new gateway. The plan also proposes a variety of distinct exterior spaces: plazas, courtyards, lawns, and roof terraces. All of these types of spaces have been realized as part of the Stata Center construction but will be expanded with the full build-out of the Northeast Sector.

Early plans and a model of the Stata Center show it in the context of the full build-out of the Northeast Sector. The architects were commissioned to provide a master plan for the sector so that the Stata Center itself could be developed with that eventual build-out in mind. The ground-floor corridor system, the landscape, and the service tunnel at the basement level are all planned to eventually connect to future building sites nearby.

Massing

To develop the massing, the design team explored many options, starting with the 1989 Wallace Floyd plan of bar buildings strung along the edge of the site (models A and B). As the process developed and the

Prior to the planning of the Stata Center, MIT had created buildings that followed a grid pattern along Vassar Street. Although the grid varied from one side to the other, it

created a wind tunnel effect and blocked natural light from penetrating the street. The 1989 Wallace Floyd plan called for an extension of this grid along Vassar Street, partly

to continue the urban pattern of the street but also to create maximum open space on campus. In developing the 1998 plan, Frank Gehry conceptualized the extension

architect came to understand more about the needs of the program, the form of the Center started to fracture into discrete elements (model C). Studies explored expansive, flat, warehouselike structures (model D) that would accommodate research projects requiring large spaces. Cruciform elements (models E and F) responded to the need for a large number of perimeter offices. Coupled with the warehouse space, the building started to form what, in the end, is a hybrid of warehouse and towers (models H, I, and J).

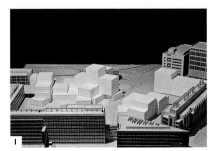
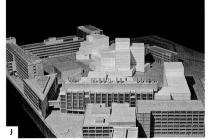

along Vassar Street very differently. Breaking up the mass of what is a very large new building on the street allows peeks of sunlight and gives definition to the building's various elements. Pulling the building back from the street near the intersection of Main and Vassar creates a more pleasant pedestrian experience. It also forms a generous outdoor space at the intersection—an open invitation to the city beyond.

The massing of the Stata Center was built from the concept of two towers sitting on a wide base referred to as a warehouse, which is essentially a hybrid of many types of buildings that Gehry's office studied. It combines the loftlike flexible spaces of a warehouse with the clustered aggregate of the towers. The marrying of these two typologies resolved a number of issues. It allowed for clear identities for components of the program as well as a variety of internal spatial arrangements. It allowed a logical breaking down of the mass of the entire building. By setting the towers on the wide two-story base, the height of the towers is

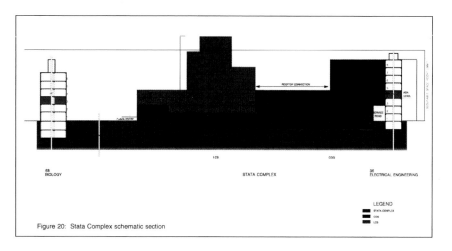

Figure 20: Stata Complex schematic section

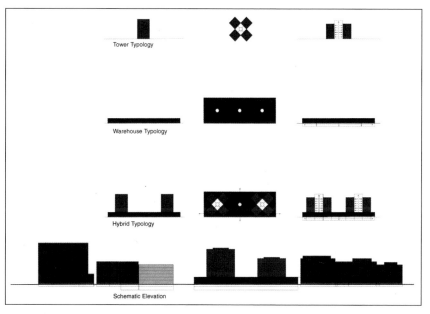

The hybrid typology of lower-level warehouse spaces for large cross-lab research endeavors, coupled with discrete towers of offices, responded to the program requirements set out by the researchers. It also made it possible to recognize the gifts of the three major donors.

minimized. This decision suggested a place for the common area central to the building—the roof of the warehouse between the towers.

Campus Connections

Traffic patterns in and around the Stata Center were carefully considered. Limited vehicular access is allowed for child-care drop-off and for MIT service vehicles (right). The infinite corridor (below left)— a continuous indoor passage linking most of MIT's academic buildings—is interrupted where vehicles need to pass between buildings. The fourth floor forms a continuous level-corridor system that is fully accessible across campus. The Stata Center continues this access by linking to Building 36 (below right).

Connections to the campus reflect the MIT tradition of openness and connectivity. The western end of the Stata Center is connected to all levels above the second floor of Building 36. The space between the buildings at these two lower levels is needed for emergency vehicle access. Building 36 houses the Electrical Engineering and Computer Science Department (EECS), and is also the home of the Research Laboratory for Electronics, which has many ties with LCS, AI,

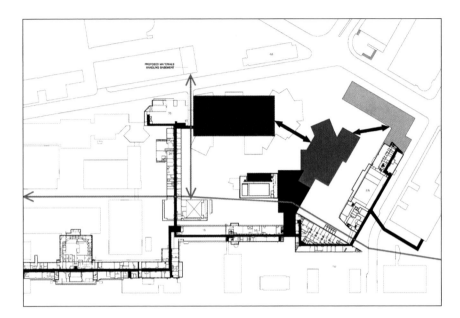

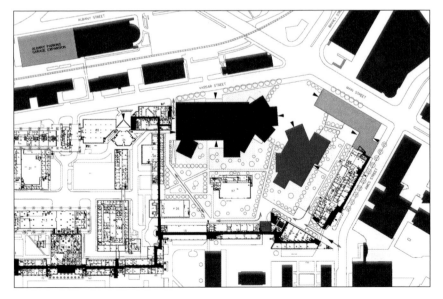

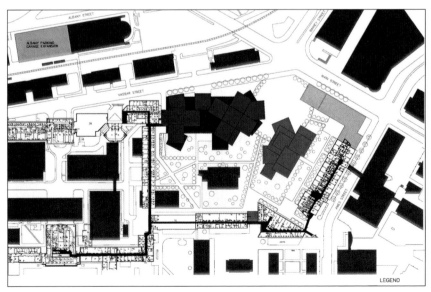

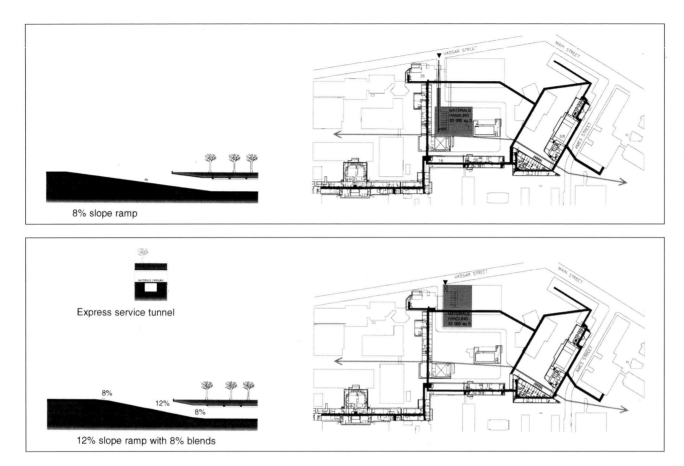

8% slope ramp

Express service tunnel

8%

12%

8%

12% slope ramp with 8% blends

As part of the conceptual plan, MIT also studied the feasibility of constructing an underground service spine for the entire campus. This service plan consists of a series of wide express tunnels with local side corridors leading to service elevators. The Stata Center has an underground shipping and receiving facility that connects to the rest of the campus through a fourteen-foot-wide tunnel. A freight elevator can deliver goods directly to the exterior for grade-level distribution.

LIDS, and L&P. In addition to the seamless transition between the research spaces of the Stata Center and Building 36, the Center is connected to the infinite corridor in many other ways. At its southwestern end, the Student Street forms an extension of the infinite corridor at grade. On the basement level, a tunnel connects to Building 26.

In a second phase, an underground corridor will extend to the east through the future Teaching and Learning Center and connect to the Biology Building. It will also loop back toward the main campus buildings at the connector between Buildings 66 and 56, where a new entrance lobby is proposed to tie the future underground corridor to

grade. This corridor will be animated by a series of major classrooms and an auditorium, and it will be punctuated with skylights in its high ceilings. The development of this eastern connection and the addition of teaching spaces will extend the cluster of instructional spaces that occupies the first floor of Building 36 and the Stata Center.

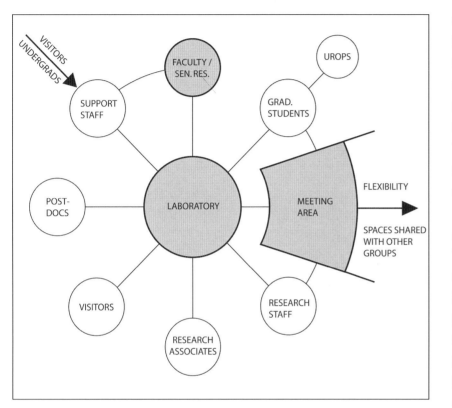

VISITORS
UNDERGRADS

FACULTY / SEN. RES.

UROPS

SUPPORT STAFF

GRAD. STUDENTS

POST-DOCS

LABORATORY

MEETING AREA

FLEXIBILITY

SPACES SHARED WITH OTHER GROUPS

VISITORS

RESEARCH STAFF

RESEARCH ASSOCIATES

To determine how to organize interior spaces, the architects developed a series of adjacency diagrams like this one, showing how different members of a group interact and the physical resources they require. Labs and meeting spaces, the focus of group activities, became the hubs around which the other spaces were organized.

Three types of work spaces emerged as part of the programming exercise for the researchers—closed spaces, flexible spaces, and preserved open spaces. Closed spaces, mostly offices, are set off by walls that will not be moved frequently. The second category, flexible spaces, may or may not be open; they will accommodate frequent change at the lab level. These are primarily research spaces. Preserved open spaces, the third category, are mostly lounges, flexible in use but fixed in location and configuration. These three types of work environments provide private space, collaborative space, and social space.

Private (Closed) Space

The offices for faculty, researchers, and graduate students make up the bulk of the private spaces in this program. Early discussions explored less traditional ways for people to be organized in the building, but in the end the private offices remained. The focus shifted to making these spaces flexible in the context of their relative permanence and encouraging people to come out of their offices to collaborate. Gehry's studies addressed the program requirement that these offices house one faculty, two staff or postdocs, or four graduate students without needing renovation.

The key was to find an office size and configuration that would accommodate four graduate students comfortably without giving over too much square footage, since one third of the offices were designated for a single faculty member.

Common criteria existed for all the office types. Each office has two distinct zones. Paperwork and computer work make up one zone, while conversation and demonstration constitute the other. A layout with a workstation, softer seating, a meeting table, and a whiteboard meets these criteria. In addition, acoustic separation, operable windows, exterior views, and visual privacy were all key criteria.

Collaborative (Flexible) Space

The programming for the research laboratories, which form the main type of collaborative space in the building and take up 40 percent of the overall square footage, became the heart of the discussions

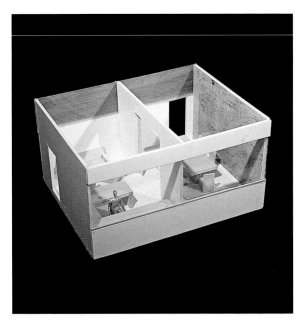

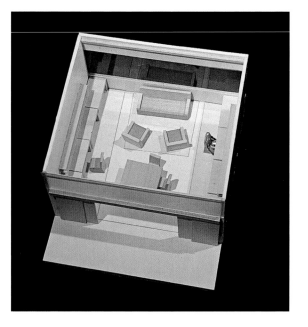

Early study models tested out the flexibility of a 200-square-foot office for use by one faculty member, two postdoctoral students, or four graduate students. The key components—office desk, personal and guest seating, meeting areas, files, shelving, and whiteboards—were all included in the test layouts.

The Japanese house scheme (left) develops the idea of communicating spaces in which configuration can quickly be changed.

A faculty office (center) includes both a private work space and a meeting space. The loft arrangement separates these functions, creating alternating levels of public, communal space and a quiet work zone.

From the shared lab space in the Orangutan Village (right), researchers ascend to their offices for more heads-down work.

between the architects and the Institute. The research groups were seen as families who lived inside a larger neighborhood of researchers. As the architects noted, "We observed a fundamental contradiction between how the users perceived their culture, from a scientist's point of view, and how we perceived it through their physical environment, from an architect's point of view. Our premise was to try to learn from the architecture of other cultures, and test out whether other ways of thinking about personal space could positively

challenge and inform the work culture of this client. Each of these cultures was selected for the legibility of its character through its architecture, a legibility which the users lack in their current environment."

Gehry's design team chose four cultures for their study, two human and two animal: the Japanese House, the Orangutan Village, the Colonial Mansion, and the Prairie Dog Town.

The Japanese House—In a traditional Japanese house, sliding screens can be configured to transform smaller private spaces into

larger open spaces. In the architect's models, several types of screens were proposed to replace fixed walls—some solid, some translucent, and some even transparent and of varying heights. The advantage of this model is its flexibility; a research group could choose how to utilize their assigned square footage.

The Orangutan Village—The analogy to this animal culture centered on the group dynamics of orangutans. At night, they ascend into the trees and build a nest for

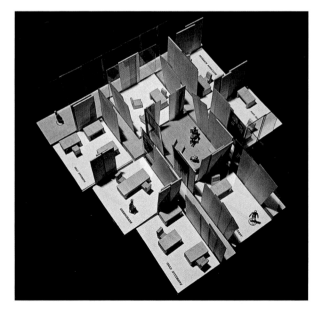

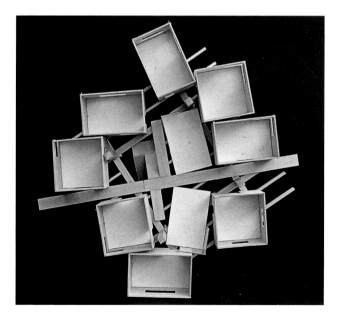

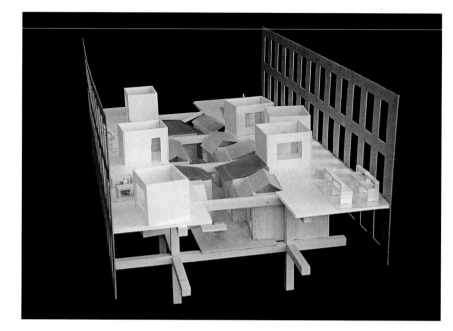

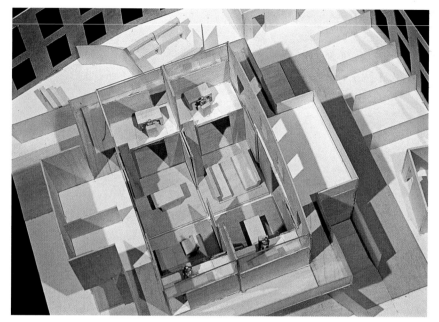

sleeping, and in the morning they descend and gather as a group. The studies that Gehry's staff conducted included a loft space inside the office, to which a faculty member could retreat for quiet study and contemplation, and a lower level for conversation or interaction with the research group or other faculty members. A further study looked at tree-house offices of a single height but sited a level higher than the lab spaces, with cracks allowing light to filter down as a tree filters light to the ground.

The Colonial Mansion—The main premise of this office layout is a fixed element with flexible areas surrounding it. Research group offices comprise the main house, which is raised, with open areas below for meeting rooms, lab spaces, and open-plan student work spaces.

The Prairie Dog Town—This plan, based on a different animal culture, is an inversion of the Orangutan Village. The private spaces lie underground, with flexible spaces

above. The "prairie" is littered with temporary structures, while the "burrows" have linear rows of offices that peek above ground through light wells.

The Prairie Dog Town (left) also divides offices and labs into separate levels. Here, the offices are densely packed into a cozy "underground" level below the open communal work spaces.

The Colonial Mansion scheme (right) preserves a mixture of closed-room and open-plan spaces.

The procedure for planning the Stata Center's overall organization reflected the planning of the group spaces. The architects tried to create positive interactions among different groups through the layout of their common physical resources.

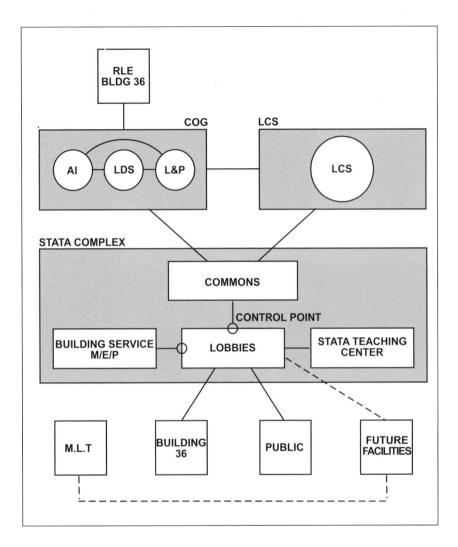

Social (Preserved Open) Space

One of the main goals of the Stata Center is to intensify interaction, cooperation, and exchange of information among its groups of researchers. To address this goal, the architects recommended the idea of a commons, very much like a town square where people naturally congregate as they go about their business. The commons (also referred to as the community center or town square) was envisioned as centrally located in the building, equally accessible to all who work there, but separated from the areas with general public access. A café and dining area, a shared reading room, seminar rooms, and an outdoor terrace facing south were suggested as components of the commons. Other social spaces in the Center include lounges in the neighborhoods and tea kitchens on each floor.

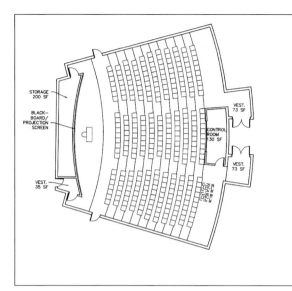

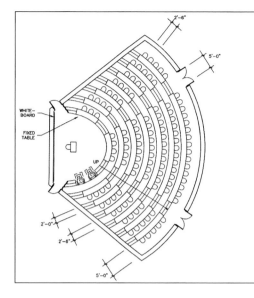

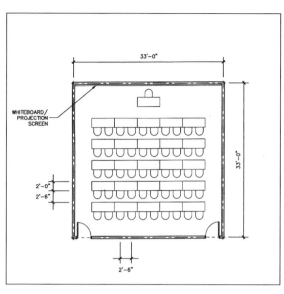

Public Space

The teaching center is one of the main components of the public space. This area will be primarily devoted to clients' graduate and undergraduate classes. The vision entailed a series of spaces—a mix of flat and tiered classrooms and a large auditorium. The capability for distance education would be part of the infrastructure, with some classrooms fitted with the appropriate equipment. The classrooms are located on the ground floor for easy access and proximity to the future

Teaching and Learning Center, which will connect to the Stata Center by way of an underground passage. A recessed auditorium was planned so that its lower entrance will tie into the underground passage.

Except for the teaching center, significant public spaces were not originally part of the Stata Center project. However, as the design evolved, the opportunity emerged to create them. Other components that came into the public program are a child-care center, a fitness center, a public food facility, the Student

Street, a library outreach program, an underground parking area, and an outdoor raised garden and amphitheater. These constitute significant additions to MIT's community infrastructure.

Determining optimal form for lecture hall and classroom spaces in the teaching center was crucial. These diagrams were the bases for discussions leading to final designs. The familiar "broadcast" lecture format (left) is still useful for large introductory classes. The challenge was to accommodate a large audience with all seats situated reasonably close to the lecturer. The ninety-seat classrooms (center) provide tables and space for spreading out materials and foster students' interaction with the lecturer and one another. The experimental classrooms (right) adapt to many teaching configurations. Traditional chalk talks, group-work tables, and workstation clusters are all possible.

Design
Collision of Ideas

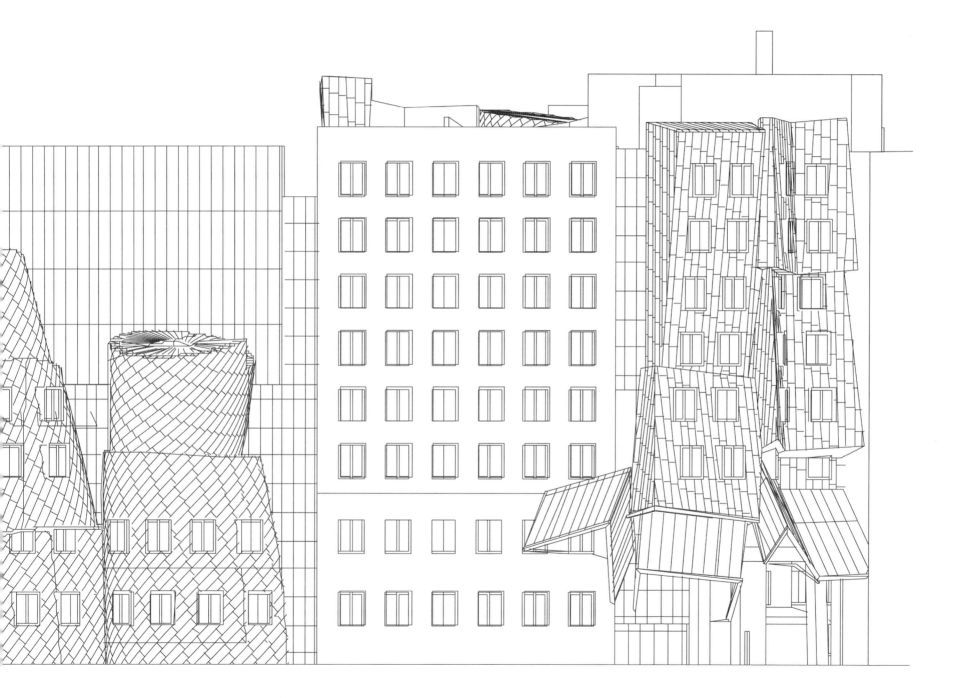

The Program Meets the Design

The crinkled paper in the model (left) denotes areas of shaping. Here, the architects have begun to experiment with wrapping the program blocks to get a sense of shaping and dynamic visual movement among the elements.

One of the early design models in the pre-schematic phase (right) utilized blocks of wood and acrylic to represent the program and adjacencies. The model starts to articulate architectural forms, blocking out tower elements and a center transition that hold common resources.

Throughout the design phase of the Ray and Maria Stata Center, the team worked hard to ensure that the building would first and foremost meet the programmatic needs set for it rather than simply form a sculptural shell with program stuffed inside. In fact, the design meets the program ably, articulating it in a sculptural framework that is distinctly Frank Gehry. The architect did not come to the project with preconceived notions of what he wanted to achieve. Rather, he listened and observed, using the results as raw material from which he developed a vision. The articulation of that

vision, the architectural expression of the Center, is very much a product of the program, the site itself, and, most important, what Gehry saw and heard and how he put it all together.

One of the major reasons that the researchers selected Gehry as architect arose after a visit to his studio. His design process seemed to match the way the researchers themselves developed their own projects. This process, heavily reliant on model making, allows ready access to the thought process behind the design. Gehry's extensive use of models—both three-

dimensional physical models and computer models—sets him apart from architects who work first in two-dimensional-sketch form and then, when the project is fully conceived, produce a presentation model. Gehry, by contrast, utilizes models from the very first breath of the creative process.

Over fifty study models, at varying scales, were developed for the Stata Center project. The first were little more than three-dimensional sketches. Wood blocks adorned with crumpled paper and other easily reconfigured material established the scale and adjacencies of the

program elements. This process continued at varying scales in order to shift perspective; in fact, the scaled study models were created through the very end of the design process.

Once the architects liked a specific model, it was digitized via CATIA. Using this computer software, an operator cleaned up the model and assigned dimensions, on which the staff based another physical model. This process happened many times over, and some models were discarded entirely. Eventually, a single base model was developed, which the designers continued to manipulate both digitally and physically throughout the design process.

Early in this process, the manip-ulations were big; whole sections of the buildings were moved around. As the design process continued, however, these adjustments became much smaller. Perhaps only the window dimensions would be modified, or, toward the very end of the design phase, a detail such as the canopy over an entrance might be refined.

CATIA is fairly new to the architectural industry. To realize their complex technical forms, Gehry's team needed technically sophisticated software capabilities that could interpret design ideas rich in three-dimensional data. To meet that need, they went to the aerospace industry's CAD market, where they discovered CATIA, which is geared toward the technical detail-ing required in airplane and automotive design.

Gehry's design process breaks down barriers that have traditionally existed between designer and client. People with little experience reading two-dimensional plans and sketches can misunderstand them and make regrettable decisions based on such miscomprehension. With the actual models in view, it is very easy to understand what works and what doesn't, and the architect is better able to explain the concepts at work and suggest alternative ways of achieving that vision.

MIT appointed a client committee constituted of researchers who would be among the initial residents in the Center. These nine people

In pre-schematics (left), connections to Building 36, the two-tower scheme, and a sense of a center space have become incorporated into the design. These elements remained and evolved with the continuing design of the Center.

An all-brick scheme (right) was modeled in response to budget concerns. Shaping is confined to the middle section and the higher areas of the building. The shaping in the middle remained and evolved with the design.

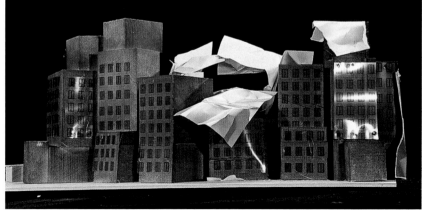

Early on, it was agreed that brick and metal would play key roles in the Stata Center. One of the models that experiments with different combinations of these materials is shown (left). Here, the entrances have begun to be articulated architecturally—a simple canopy for the Dreyfoos Building and an extension beyond the Gates Building. The service entrance also shows up as a simple rectangular block.

In the model that represented the end of schematic design (right), the size and forms of the building are in place, the entrances are well defined, the sizes and basic number of windows are indicated, and the intent for creating a microclimate is articulated by a large glass roof. Cost prohibited the glass roof from moving beyond schematics, however.

became part of the project management structure and spent a great deal of time reacting to the various design options presented by the architects. Budget was a crucial consideration, and manipulating the physical models allowed everyone to immediately visualize the impact of budget-driven choices. Along with Gehry's cost-estimating process, these models also helped maintain awareness of the budgetary consequences of specific design decisions.

In developing the program for the building, the researchers laid out specific goals that they were determined to preserve. Their diligence set up a creative tension that ultimately balanced architectural expression and interior program.

In fact, much of the architectural expression itself arose from the architect's conversations with the researchers.

The building is set up as a two-level warehouse platform topped by two towers. The idea of the warehouse space came from the researchers, who wanted flexible, open labs with high ceilings that could be easily reconfigured and combined with adjoining labs for large-scale projects. The two towers break up the mass of the large building and provide separate identities for the labs and departments. Inside, the towers are folded into research group–size wings, with more visual separation yet without actual barriers. The massing of the

wings also creates more exterior surface, which satisfies the goal for all the offices to receive natural light. The roof of the warehouse that lies between the towers unifies the towers and the warehouse. Here, on the fourth and fifth levels, the researchers opted to combine program space into a kind of town square, which provides meeting and socializing opportunities, both indoors and out.

The Stata Center is organized as a series of steps from public to private. At the ground-floor level, space is available for public use. Outside, rising up through a wide stair-ramp on the south side or an outdoor amphitheater on the east side, a raised exterior garden

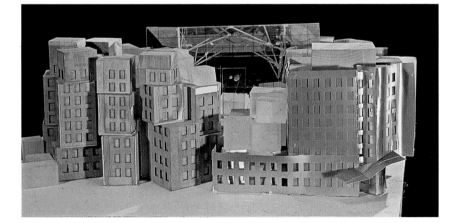

provides the MIT community with outdoor furniture and plantings oriented toward the south. Above this garden, however, the building starts to become more private. This is expressed architecturally and, in some cases, through actual security barriers.

Access to the town square is gained via two generous flights of stairs overlooking light courts, with views down into the warehouse labs. Doorways that can be closed off discourage casual visitors from entering to reach these stairs, however. Above this level, research floors are accessed either through closed stairwells or elevators that open onto lobbies that can be secured. Small outdoor porches or terraces are available on some of these levels. This sequence of lower-level public spaces to increasingly private upper-floor spaces addresses the goals of the researchers, who wanted to provide places for interaction among the faculty and research population and the undergraduate and general MIT community while maintaining the security and privacy necessary for effective research and collaboration.

The design of the Stata Center held the researchers' program sacred, but it also met MIT's goals by defining the project as one piece in a much larger, campuswide puzzle. Site constraints, service needs, maintenance concerns, plans for other buildings, and undergraduate and community populations all had to be considered. As well as it met many of the challenges posed by the researchers, the Stata Center design also met those set by the Institute. For example, the connections to Building 36, the existing Alumni Pool, and Building 26, and planned connections to the future build-out of the entire Northeast Sector define the Stata Center as a continuation of the infinite corridor. The creation of an underground shipping and receiving center allows the addition of significant green space and pedestrian pathways to the sector. The ground-level cafeteria, fitness center, and interior Student Street, with classrooms and an auditorium, have transformed this

The final shaping and the mixing of the brick and metal materials have started to settle down in this model. Design changes are now smaller as the model heads to the end of design development.

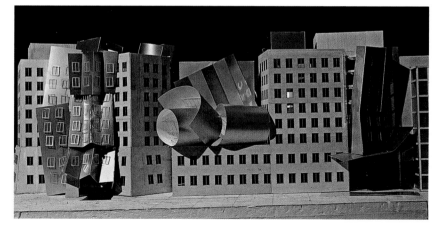

Variations in the volumes along the Student Street provide space for large-scale graphic panels, whiteboards, and displays. Information about campus events is mounted on the display boards, while the whiteboards encourage intellectual exchange of ideas in a casual and communal setting. The graphic panels are made of open mesh. Ranging from six by eight feet to nine by twelve feet, these panels are meant to be changed occasionally, thus setting an ever-changing backdrop to the activities along the Student Street.

sector of campus into a destination point for many undergraduate students.

Gehry's challenge—one he was very eager to take up—was to tackle a complex set of program requirements. With multiple users and conflicting needs, a consensus-driven design process, a restricted budget, and a mundane urban site, the challenge was daunting. A project like this—a bit edgy and certainly outside MIT business as usual—is certain to have its detractors. But as the project has come to realization, as the brilliance of Gehry's vision has unveiled itself in

the construction process, many doubts have dissipated.

Because this project was being designed for a group of technologically sophisticated people, the architects were interested in exploring some innovative design solutions. Early in the project they looked at emerging technologies from some of MIT's own labs to see if any could be incorporated into the project. They also explored technologies being used in Europe, where environmental criteria are more stringent than those of the United States. Many avenues were explored and not pursued, but some were integrated into the project, and this process of exploration set the tone for project team members, who were encouraged to be creative and loose, to collaborate openly, to take chances when making recommendations. This environment fostered technical innovations large and small. When the slurry wall was being designed, for example, instead of taking the conservative route of tying the slurry wall to bedrock, the geotechnical engineer conducted a series of calculations

based on knowledge of the site, borings taken at the time, and advice from an MIT professor. Together with the contractor, they came up with a recommendation that saved the project more than $2 million and cut time from the schedule.

During utilities installation, instead of shutting down the twenty-inch chilled-water lines, the contractor recommended "hot tapping" the line, a procedure normally done only on pipes of much smaller diameters. This process also saved money but, more important, it saved the Institute from interrupting service to the many research labs that relied on the chilled water.

To address the researchers' programmatic goal of spatial flexibility, the mechanical engineers recommended an under-floor displacement system, in one of the first applications of this process in this country. Not only does this system save energy, but it also eliminates the need for extensive ceiling ductwork and system rework during future renovations. The installation of a raised floor also opened up the

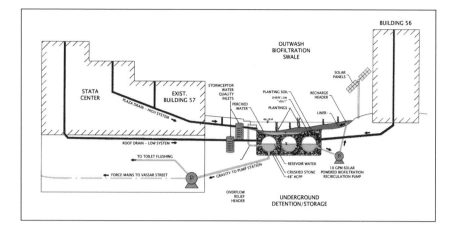

opportunity to install a modular electrical system, which adds to the flexible infrastructure.

Discussions about the exterior of the building led to a consideration of European double-wall glass systems. Although pursuing this was not cost effective, the research led to a decision to create a micro-climate so that the outdoors could be enjoyed for more of the year. The architects achieved this by wrapping the building around a series of out-door terraces.

Perhaps one of the more exciting innovations is the storm-water man-agement system, developed in con-junction with the landscape plan for the Northeast Sector. This dry creek bed collects rainwater from adjoin-ing roofs and surrounding plazas and retains it in a series of under-ground collection cells. This water is filtered through plantings and crushed stone. Then it is either sent to a holding tank inside the building to be used as gray water for flushing toilets or sent to the city's main drainage system. The pumps are powered by solar panels.

The landscape plan itself is a real departure from what MIT denizens are used to seeing on cam-pus. Because the Institute sits on coastal land, the campus is essen-tially flat. Envisioning New England hillsides, the landscape architect suggested bringing a little inland topography to the site. The final design for the build-out of the entire Northeast Sector shows drumlins with plantings, a pond that rises and falls with the tide, and south-facing raised terraces brought up into the sunlight and protected from wind by the buildings themselves.

A diagrammatic section through the site (left) illustrates the storm-water-manage-ment system. Rainwater from surrounding buildings and run-off from the Stata Center are collected, filtered, and either reused or sent out to the city's storm-water system. The landscape scheme (right) envisions planted drumlins as tall as nine feet and a series of raised terraces.

Exterior Design

The final design model, at one-quarter-inch scale, measured approximately eight feet by twelve feet and rose three feet high. The Gates and Dreyfoos Buildings, separated by the white aluminum-clad Twins, make up the Vassar Street facade. The Twins serve both as a transition between the two buildings and an evocation of the church steeples of New England. Early in the design, the architect proposed incorporating two glass domes, one at each building, to give the Center a tie-in with the more classic domes of the Main Group. Although the building is structured to receive them in the future, these domes are not part of the final design.

The Ray and Maria Stata Center comprises two buildings, the William H. Gates and the Alexander W. Dreyfoos Buildings, which combine rectangular brick towers with sculptural, metal-clad elements. Within the towers, each research neighborhood is anchored by a rectangular wing clad in brick and lined with modular offices. These modular offices alternate with areas of distinctively shaped offices clad on the exterior in metal. In both towers, these areas are organized around a central glazed light court, which looks across an outdoor terrace to the other tower. The two towers together form a C-shape, providing a protective south-facing outdoor environment.

The Center was designed to be porous. Pedestrians approach the building from many directions, and entrances are placed to receive these traffic flows. Each building has a separate entrance at grade level on Vassar Street. These entrances are covered with canopies fashioned from a combination of tinted titanium and stainless steel. The use of titanium in the canopies distinguishes them from the cladding treatment on other parts of the building. At the west end, where traffic flows primarily from Building 36 and the child-care drop-off area, ground-floor doors open to the Dreyfoos Building lobby and the Student Street. Two separate openings from the south side allow direct entrance to the Student Street.

On the campus side of the building, between the Stata Center and the existing Alumni Pool, a raised garden has been created for the MIT community, providing a generous park setting for relaxation, recreation, and study. Trees, benches, and pedestrian pathways articulate smaller-scale spaces. An exterior elevator, a generous set of stairs, and an amphitheater all provide access to this garden. It can also be approached from the interior of the building through two entrance points. The amphitheater is an open-air, semicircular seating area that accommodates 350 people. Studded with shade trees, the amphitheater can be used for informal lectures, performances, or—most of the time —a casual gathering space.

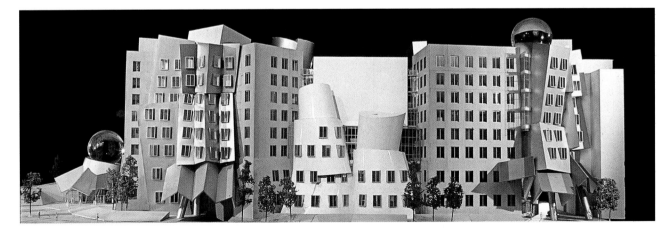

Early in the design discussions, Frank Gehry used the Château de Chambord in France as an example of the imagery he envisioned for the terrace (left). Like the château, although on a more modest scale, the Stata Center has a large terrace set with building elements sized to create the scale of a cityscape. The blue cylindrical element at lower left (to be built later) is an extension of the child-care center. The area is now used as a playground.

Other outdoor spaces grace the Stata Center. Overlooking the raised garden, for example, a smaller upper terrace is the focus of the Community Center on the fourth floor. Seminar rooms for each department encircle this protected exterior space, which is punctuated by a café, the roof of which bears yet another outdoor space. This upper terrace is connected to a sculpted conference room that is intended for special gatherings.

The Stata Center was built primarily of flat reinforced concrete slabs and columns. Concrete as a material responds well to the type of shaping that Frank Gehry proposed for the exterior of the

building. While most columns are vertical, the geometry of some of the building elements required that some of the columns be slightly tilted in some areas. And, in a few cases, the columns act in tension, supporting a slab from above. The building elements that surround the upper terrace are framed in steel. These objects rest on the third-floor slab, are separate visually from the

towers, and consist of highly shaped structures that house spaces that may stand two or more stories high.

The enclosure of the exterior walls uses two different siding materials, metal and brick, which are in many places bridged with glass to articulate building shapes, thereby breaking down the scale of the Stata Center. In general, the simple massive blocks of the Gates

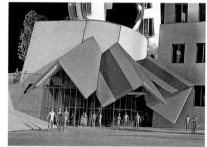

The raised terrace (above, left) is flanked by seminar rooms and social spaces that give definition to the outdoor terrace, which is protected by a vertical barrier called the wind wall.

Two entrances—the Gates (above, center) and the Dreyfoos (right)—front Vassar Street. Each is articulated by large overhanging canopies clad with ribbons of tinted titanium.

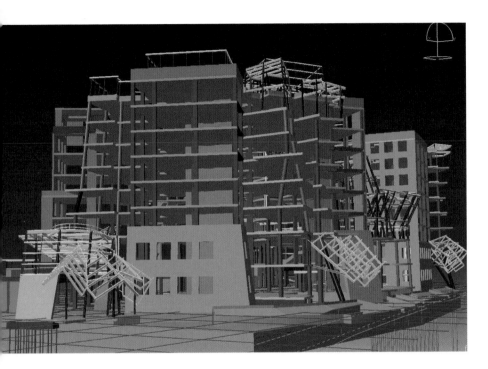

and Dreyfoos Buildings are clad in brick, as are other blocklike elements such as the auditorium, the café, and the Star. The various roof terraces are also finished in brick, creating a seamless transition from horizontal to vertical. To further break down the scale of the Center, both the Gates and Dreyfoos Buildings are recessed at least once over the height of the structure. These setbacks create ledges and roofs of various depths, which, again, are paved in brick or stainless to bestow a monolithic appearance on the buildings' facades.

The windows in the metal facade are stainless-steel cantilevered units, each adapted to the various sculptural shapes and facets. Except for the Star, which is clad in brick, all the upper-terrace elements are finished in metal, largely stainless steel with an angel-hair finish. The mirror finish on the Nose, however, differentiates it from the other sculptural spaces on the terrace. By contrast, the Kiva and the Helmet are finished in painted aluminum.

One fundamental objective of the program was to permit natural light to penetrate into the building

The concrete structure comprised flat slabs and columns, except for areas that needed to resist sheer, where the concrete is formed up as walls.

The color of the brick contributes to the sheen taken on by the adjacent stainless steel (right); the tone changes with the time of day and amount of cloud cover.

A cutaway (far right)—which cannot be seen in the finished building—shows the play among brick, metal, and glass.

as deeply as possible. The glazing elements that accomplish this take on various forms. For example, the office modules, which comprise a large part of the program, are organized along the perimeter of the building and alternate with open lab and office spaces. Large windows punctuate these program spaces—flat window units in the brick building components and projecting windows in the metal. Glass curtain-wall elements articulate transitions between brick and metal by spanning the sculptural voids between them. The largest glass walls and roofs are located around the upper terrace, where they create visual connection between research neighborhoods and common spaces. Other glass elements include a glass roof that covers the central part of the Student Street and a series of skylights that bring light into the athletic facility, the teaching spaces, the upper floors of the towers, and the warehouse level.

Interior Design

The Center's interior encourages the play between public and private spaces, between zones conducive to deep contemplation and to intellectual and social interaction. The architecture supports this by visual clues—wide, open staircases and views beyond enhance the social zones, small meeting areas form a space between public and private zones, and private offices are clustered away from social areas to facilitate quiet work. On the upper levels, private and shared offices hug the naturally lit exterior walls, and research labs and small informal meeting spaces fill up the interior spaces. On the lower levels this arrangement is reversed. The private and shared offices take up the interior, and the labs and meeting spaces benefit from the natural light. On all levels, the shared facilities, such as conference rooms, tea kitchens, and lounges, are situated closer to the elevators and staircases. This arrangement creates an efficient floor plate by minimizing the public corridors needed to access these shared spaces.

Connections between the labs on the warehouse levels are visually open, facilitating collaborative work. The towers are organized as a series of two-story neighborhoods, and common lounges connect the levels with an open spiral stair.

On the ground floor, the entrances to the Stata Center lead to the Student Street. This indoor circulation path widens, with a series of alcoves along its edges. Conveniences such as vending machines, telephones, automatic teller machines, information kiosks, seating areas, and

The generous public stair to the fourth-floor commons is surrounded by light and views. Skylights let in natural light, and the glass area punctures adjoining research labs.

student club booths are accommodated along the path and in the alcoves. In addition, the Student Street acts as a spine from which many other activity spaces are accessed, including the teaching center, which is made up of a large lecture hall, two tiered classrooms, and two experimental classrooms. These five spaces are used primarily by MIT's School of Engineering. They are designed to promote innovative teaching methods in a friendly learning environment that integrates the latest technology without forfeiting the human interactions characteristic of MIT's academic program. Other activity spaces include a new athletic facility connected to the Alumni Pool, a cafeteria and café, library services, an information desk and retail outlet, exhibit space, and a child-care facility for children of faculty, students, and staff.

The Student Street also leads to other areas in the building. Through a naturally lit atrium, wide stairs and elevators provide access to a lower-level academic hub with tutoring services, an advanced technology classroom, and a homeroom for fifth-year engineering students. And below this hub, accessed from the same central atrium, is a two-level, 685-car underground parking facility. The Student Street also boasts a set of sculptural stairs at each end. These stairs lead up to the two basic research areas—the warehouse neighborhood and the tower neighborhood.

The warehouse, located on levels two and three, combines a deep and wide continuous floor with fifteen-foot-high ceilings. Shared by the newly merged Lab of Computer Science and Artificial Intelligence (CSAIL), it is intended to attract research groups that require a large laboratory volume, both vertically and horizontally. To allow natural light to penetrate these deep floors, a number of private and shared offices have been placed in the interior.

The offices have tall glass clerestories and sidelights to share the natural light. The two warehouse levels receive abundant natural light through two large light courts, a central skylight, and the glass roofs covering the Student Street. The warehouse neighborhoods share common areas such as a lounge and conference rooms located inside enclosed spaces seated under the light courts.

The typical tower neighborhood, which links two floors, combines single- and double-height spaces. The offices line most of the perimeter; the shared spaces and circulation area occupy the center of the floor, and the two-story lounge visually connects to the central upper terrace and the opposite tower through a floor-to-ceiling glass wall. Larger lab spaces flank the lounges, sharing the glass wall, while the smaller ones are internal spaces at the center of each wing.

Despite its rather complex appearance from the exterior, the internal organization of the Stata Center is fairly simple. Activities needing privacy or acoustic and visual separation are housed away from the common and collaborative spaces; public areas are readily accessible, but their boundaries discourage random wandering. Frank Gehry's challenge was to provide spaces that protect researchers from

interruptions while maintaining an open campus environment, where people are encouraged to interact intellectually and socially.

After researching a number of conventional and nonconventional systems to deliver heat and cooling, the design engineers recommended a displacement air system, which has many advantages over conventional ceiling systems. Typically, ceiling systems deliver air at a height and velocity that create a mixing effect. The air supply for displacement ventilation, however, supplies air from the floor at low velocity, which displaces the warmer air in the room. This process maintains the supply temperature only slightly below the desired room temperature, an energy savings that will accrue to the Institute over the operational life of the system. Heat and contaminants produced by activities in the room are also displaced and removed by exhaust vents near the ceiling, thereby improving the air quality.

The system configuration also allows individuals to control temperature levels in offices and meeting

areas. Instead of individual variable-air-volume boxes, each room has motorized dampers at each floor grille zoned separately at a much smaller cost. The grille can easily be rotated to redirect air; however, the low velocity of air circulation means that there is little perception of its movement. Also, opening and closing the windows affects only the individual room's temperature. A long-term advantage to the system is its ease of reconfiguration. Because there is no ductwork under the floor and the cavity itself acts as

Offices are simple expressions of the way researchers work. The typical office accommodates a desk, places for meeting, shelving, natural light, and operable windows.

facing page:
Two-story lounge areas hug the exterior glass facades in both towers. These lounges connect a two-story neighborhood, providing visual connection across the two towers through a continuous wall of glazing and light.

A computer model of a typical south-facing office (top) mimics the natural light that would penetrate into the space, with no shading, on a sunny September afternoon.

False-color technology used in the same office model (bottom) results in calculation of luminence, or brightness, that exceeds desired levels. Congenial work conditions for computer use require that no screen reflection is visible and luminence is fairly even.

facing page:
Light studies in the research villas, under the light courts, modeled different times of day and different seasons to determine what types of shading devices would be most effective. The challenge was to integrate control devices that solve problems of glare and solar radiation while maintaining the transparent character of the space.

the duct, the floor damper and grille can be relocated easily.

In a computer research facility, sufficient electrical capacity and efficient distribution are essential. The raised floor and displacement air system create an ideal distribution path for electrical power. The mechanical system is highly flexible. The power flows to main distribution ports and then branches off to a series of secondary distribution ports. Spare ports are built into the system to accommodate future use, and all components are "plug and play," so that adding or relocating is easy. The outlets are distributed either to the walls through a short, flexible cable or to a floor box. They, too, are movable.

Perhaps the second most important capacity in a computer science building is data connectivity. MIT provides basic service for both phone and data to all its buildings, and the researchers also use data as part of their research activity. Both networks have been installed under the floor, although distributed separately. For the researchers' use, the building also has an overhead cable-tray system that allows easy access to add on or change out data configurations as research needs change. To make efficient use of this tray, the lighting fixtures along the corridors are integrated into the data cable system.

Another program requirement was to allow an abundance of natural light to penetrate into the interior of the building. But daylight is perceived differently, depending on weather conditions and the time of year. Though it does not provide the high-quality, consistent level of lighting needed in a work environment, its special qualities make it highly desirable. At the same time, it can compromise computer use and video projection.

The natural light in the Stata Center comes from windows, skylights, light courts, and other glazed openings. To help control the light, shading devices reduce glare and solar radiation; in some cases, they block the light entirely. Artificial lighting and daylight combine to meet the variety of lighting needs in the building. The sources of artificial lighting vary, depending on the use of a given space. The ceiling grid is populated with potential locations for light fixtures. This grid was formed into the concrete underslab to accommodate whatever type of hung lighting is desired. At this time pendant lights hang in the open offices and laboratories, and offices have indirect, side-mounted fixtures. Supplemental task lighting provides individual control of light levels in both of these areas.

The Teaching Center

The Lecture Hall—The 350-seat auditorium is arranged in three seating groups served by two aisles. A crossover zone at the back also serves as a handout distribution point. The front of the auditorium is equipped with sliding chalkboards and roll-down screens as well as a complete sound system, with microphone jacks built in at the front and in four locations in the auditorium. The audiovisual systems may be controlled either from the projection room at the rear or from the instructor's workstation. The skylight is equipped with a complete shading system that permits both diffusion of light and blackout.

The three types of lecture venues on the Student Street—auditorium (left), tiered classroom (right), and experimental teaching space (center)—all have perforated-wood paneling on the walls; in the auditorium, this paneling extends to the ceiling. The auditorium and the west tiered lecture room are equipped with distance learning capabilities. All classrooms can receive broadcasts and are equipped with pathways for future enhancements. A fourth type of classroom planned for the Stata Center—a TEAL (technology-enabled active-learning) classroom—will be located on the concourse level, along with other student learning spaces.

Tiered classrooms—These two fan-shaped rooms, equipped with fixed tables and movable chairs, accommodate ninety people each. Two aisles serve a maximum of five seats in a row; a crossover zone in the back provides a location for leaving handouts. Screens and chalkboards are situated at the front, with audiovisual control at the podium. Although the room is designed to accommodate unamplified speech, distributed ceiling speakers are also available when needed. Natural light streams through a skylight or a glass roof, and a clerestory permits additional illumination to enter from the Student Street. A complete shading system permits precise control over the level of this light.

Experimental classrooms—The raised flat floor in these two fifty-seat classrooms provides a flexible seating configuration and access to many points of under-floor power and data. The chalkboards are located on two walls, while an overhead grid provides a mounting surface for movable screens and audiovisual elements. The control workstation is also movable, equipped with an "umbilical cord" that can plug into any point on the floor. Natural light pours in from the clerestory and can be controlled by shading devices.

Student and Community Spaces

The Student Street—The Student Street is a skylit interior public arcade intended for use by the MIT community, especially undergraduate students. Activity tables, mail kiosks, vending machines, and informal seating areas offer opportunities for meetings, social interaction, and information sharing in a visually vibrant environment.

Athletic Center and Alumni Pool—Underneath the raised garden and connected to the existing Alumni Pool, the Stata Center provides the MIT community with a new athletic facility. New and updated locker rooms, a fitness center with weight training and aerobics machines, a flexible dance studio with a floating wood floor, and direct connections to the existing pool are the principal components of this new facility.

The Child-Care Center—A new center for children is included in the program for the Stata Center. This center, housing sixty-five children ranging from infants to prekindergarten age, is designed for flexibility. If there is a change in the ratio of infants to toddlers, for instance, the classroom can accommodate the shift with little renovation. The classrooms are organized into village clusters, each accommodating seven to ten children, with their own kitchen and bathroom facilities. Common play spaces for the different age groups, an adjacent outdoor playground, and a drop-off area for parents complete the configuration.

The Café—The 150-seat food facility is open for full service during meal hours and as a café after hours. Access is provided to computer networks and the Internet. During late-night operating hours, library personnel are on hand to assist students in accessing electronic media for research. As part of this service, the library has a small meeting room equipped with whiteboards and projection capabilities.

Research Areas

The Commons—Social connectivity between labs and departments is accomplished by creating a community at the intersection of the warehouse and the towers at the

heart of the Center. This town square assembles most of the large meeting and social spaces, housing three seminar rooms, an extensive display area, a common copy facility, and a large central multipurpose space that is used for faculty dining during the day and as a pub and space for graduate student–faculty social interaction in the afternoon and evening. These rooms surround the upper terrace, a south-facing outdoor space that becomes a meeting place itself.

Villas—Two three-story enclosed interior spaces within the light courts of the east and west towers could be described as "buildings

Three views of the Student Street demonstrate the variety and vitality of the space: varying heights and sloping elements pierce through the skylights (left); an intimate dining area with abundant natural light (right) has views into programmed areas; and sweeping stairs provide overlooks in addition to passage (center).

Similar sets of resources are found on every research floor (right): private offices, open single- and double-height labs for work that can be visually shared, segregated labs for work that may require light or noise control, and shared rooms for meetings and socializing.

Tall atriumlike research spaces (below) house a variety of activities. The labs provide height for experiments that require tall spaces, such as those involving autonomous aircraft.

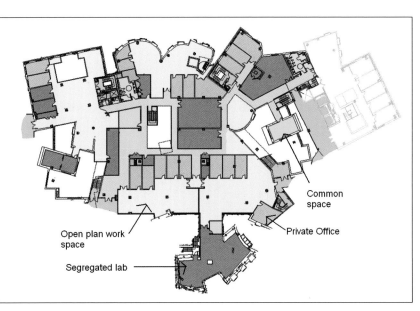

Common space

Open plan work space

Private Office

Segregated lab

within a building." These villas, which include offices, conference rooms, and lounge areas, provide a sense of scale to the light courts and diffuse natural light. Their vibrant colors animate the areas around them.

Neighborhoods—The laboratory research groups are based on the idea of neighborhoods. And like any neighborhood, they are made up of a variety of private and public spaces and communal resources that give the neighborhood individual character. The laboratory neigh-

borhoods include faculty offices, shared offices, open and segregated labs, and open work spaces for graduate students, which together make up the private and collaborative spaces. Each floor has communal resources such as a tea kitchen, a copy machine alcove, restrooms, conference rooms, and informal small meeting nooks outfitted with a whiteboard and a couple of chairs.

The neighborhood is a two-story unit, a scheme that is intended to expand on the more typical, strictly linear arrangement in order to allow more flexibility in configuring the

size of the research group. The floors are connected by double-height lounges with an open and inviting spiral stair.

The lounges, positioned centrally, are open and visible to people as they step out of the elevator lobbies. Views to the exterior orient people as they enter the floor. The lounges also look across the terrace, making a visual connection between the towers across the open span.

Although the warehouse neighborhoods stretch out horizontally to take advantage of the large continuous floor area, their organization is similar to the tower neighborhoods, with private offices and shared offices grouped around open and segregated labs, sharing common resources.

Research laboratories—Collaborative research environments are designed to serve ten to fifteen people each, the size of the basic research group. Group areas are homey, providing a sense of group identity while encouraging collaboration. They are clearly marked, either through architectural expression or a physical barrier such as a door, thus discouraging outsiders from entering but encouraging interaction among neighbors.

Two types of laboratories are provided: segregated and open-space labs. Each has its own specific architectural vocabulary. A segregated lab may be isolated acoustically and visually from surrounding activities; some are equipped with full-height partitions and limited-access doors in order to protect expensive equipment.

Labs that need some security but not isolation are outfitted with dividing walls: exposed heavy-gauge steel studs act as hanging devices to accommodate a variety of panel types, which create a physical barrier but allow light and air to pass freely through at various heights. The interior architecture is meant to be open, with uninterrupted views and well-marked pathways. Allowing a maximum of light to travel into and through laboratories preserves both views and pathways.

Offices—The design of the Stata Center began with the design of the

offices. Models in various scales were created to explore size and functionality, culminating in full-scale mock-ups of a warehouse office and a tower office.

Many of the early programmatic goals—abundant natural light and air, good acoustic separation, and flexibility—influenced design decisions. For example, the desire for natural light in all offices led to an exploration of many exterior surfaces. The need for flexibility led to a typical module office size of 200 square feet, which can accommodate one faculty member, two researchers, or four graduate students. This goal also led to design-

ing a raised-floor system that houses all mechanical and electrical distribution.

Of the approximately 350 offices in the building, most hug the exterior. In the warehouse spaces, however, the large continuous floor area necessitates the inclusion of some interior rooms.

Double-height labs (left) are meant to foster communication between floors. Typically placed along an exterior wall, they distribute natural light deep into the building. They are also situated next to an open and inviting stairwell, suffused with natural light. The stairwell does double duty as an emergency exit.

A double-height lounge (right) connects its two-story neighborhood by means of an internal stair. These tower lounges are located along the exterior glass-curtain wall, providing a glowing face that can be seen from the opposite tower.

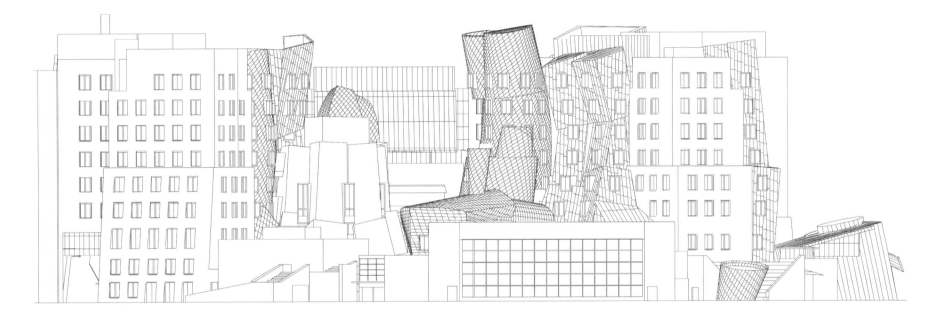

Compton Court Elevation

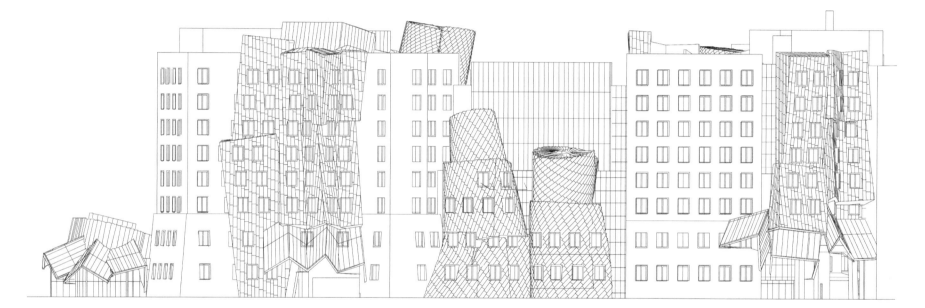

Vassar Street Elevation

Gates Building Elevation

Dreyfoos Building Elevation

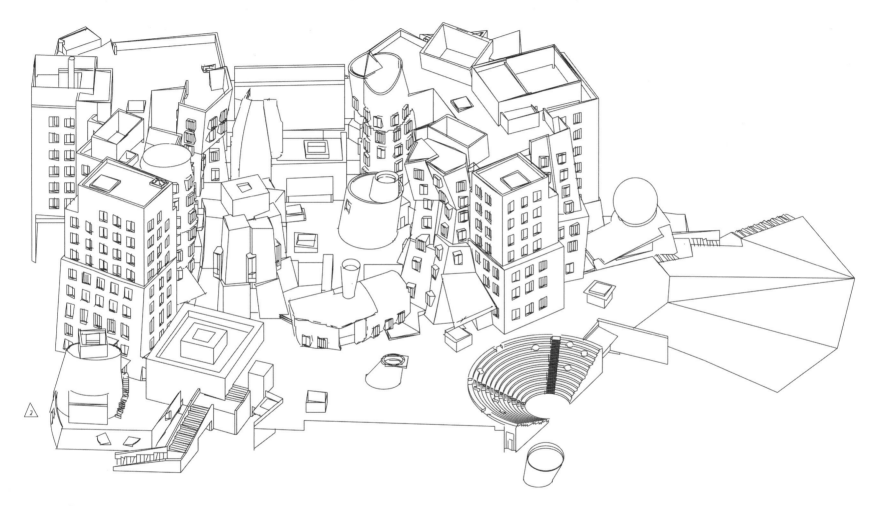

South View

BUILDING STATA

North View

West View

BUILDING STATA

East View

Levels 1 and 2

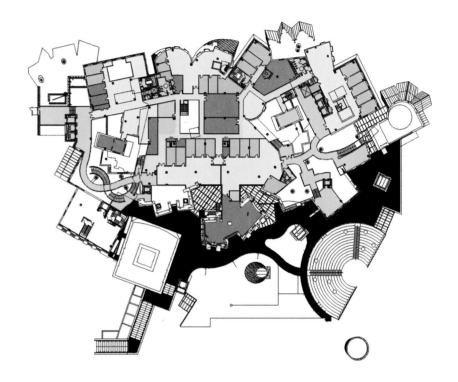

Level 3

Office

Open-Plan

Segregated Lab

Common

Client Circulation

Public Circulation

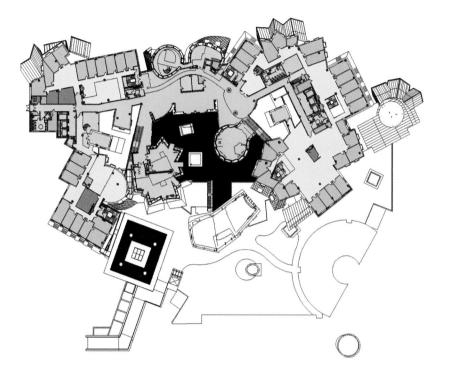

Level 4

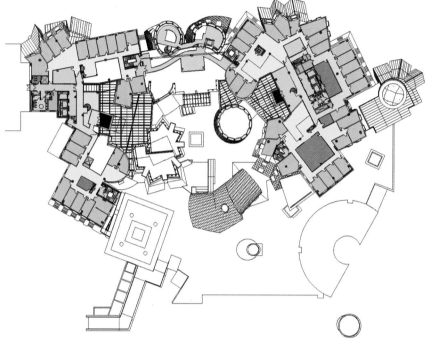

Level 5

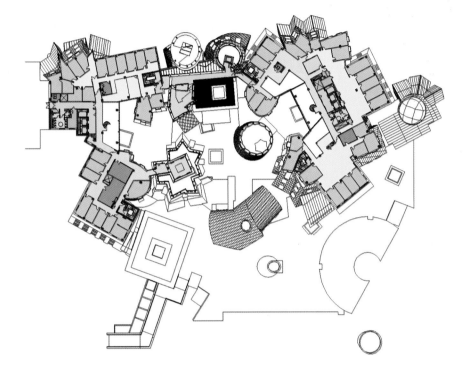

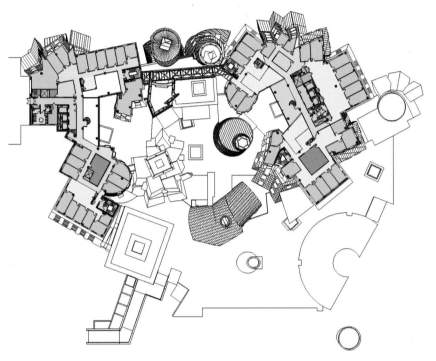

Level 6

Level 7

Office

Open-Plan

Segregated Lab

Common

Client Circulation

Public Circulation

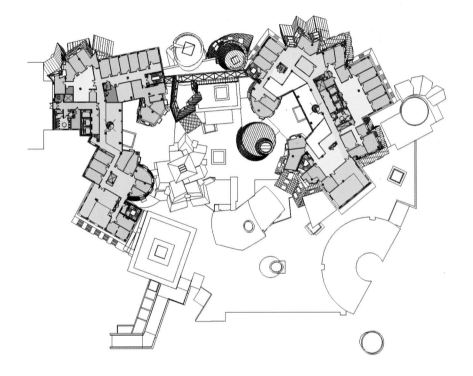

Level 8

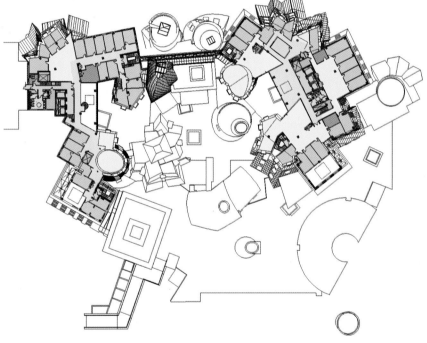

Level 9

Construction

Means, Methods, and Materials

The Design Meets the Construction

Construction activities take many forms. These divergent activities all are necessary parts of the construction process, from a meeting at the metal fabricator's shop that included the architect, builder, owner, and subcontractor (left), to an on-site crew accessing areas of the building by means of temporary construction stairs in a specific sector of the site (center), to workers reviewing a set of shop drawings (right).

Once Frank Gehry was selected to be the architect for the new Stata Center, MIT assembled a team to support the design of this facility. Gehry's nontraditional approach to design and construction and the location of his firm's headquarters—Los Angeles—led the Institute to bring on a construction company early in the process. Gehry Partners not only concurred with this decision but also felt strongly that this company should ultimately become the builder of the Center to ensure ownership of preconstruction advice.

The Institute put together a set of criteria, with the architect's advice and input, to guide the search for a construction firm. A prime criterion was that the company have sufficient financial backing to take on a project of this size. MIT also sought a company that knew the local labor market, had longstanding relations with subcontractors, and had worked successfully with the Institute in the past. By the time these deliberations took place, Gehry had completed several significant projects overseas, so MIT also looked for a company

that had international resources and was familiar with European technology. In hiring Gehry's firm, the Institute was well aware that innovative design and prominent use of computer technology were in the offing and a good match indeed for many of the building's occupants—computer science researchers whose work focuses on innovation and cutting-edge technology. To complete the team, the Institute wanted a construction company proficient in technology usage, able to support experimental design proposals, and

possessing the intellectual depth to actively participate in potentially esoteric discussions early in the design process.

All of these criteria, it turned out, were met by Beacon Skanska Construction Company (currently named Skanska USA Building, Inc.). Beacon was a local firm that had merged with the Swedish company Skanska USA a number of years before the start of this project. In Skanska, MIT got the best of both worlds—a local company that had long relationships with and deep knowledge of the local construction community as well as the financial backing and

international expertise expected of one of the largest construction companies in the world. In addition, Skanska's president at the time, Jim Becker, was a former member of the MIT faculty. His intimate knowledge of the Institute's internal culture and its academic mission, coupled with the company's recent work there, ensured good representation during the design of the Center.

During the design phase, Skanska provided support for design explorations, focusing on system and material options, cost, schedule, and construction methods. As the design evolved, the company identified key subcontractors, some of whom they

engaged to provide advice about design details and cost. Early in the process, the architect and the Institute explored some research projects then under way at MIT to see if an application might be included as part of the design and construction. For example, the team considered new lighting technology, ways to capture and reuse heat from computer CPUs, and some visual graphic tools being developed by the computer scientists themselves. The builder's role was to provide construction feasibility analysis and estimates of cost. Much of this discussion was academic in nature, and the builder had to translate

Tools of construction run the gamut from ironworkers' hand tools in the field to shop drawings in the field office.

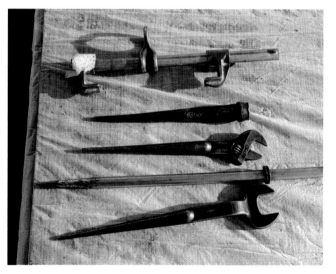

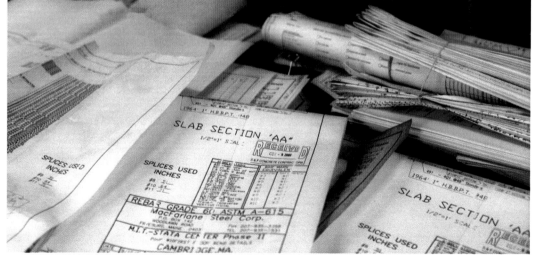

abstract notions into real dollars and cents. In the end, none of these projects had arrived at a market stage, but the conversations they inspired encouraged the entire team to think creatively about light, heat, and the use of computers in the building.

Many of the assemblies installed in the Stata Center were developed specifically for this project, requiring custom design and fabrication and, in some cases, custom installation techniques. This presented significant challenges for both the

MIT was competing with the Big Dig for skilled tradespeople. Bidding for the project took place in 2000 and 2001, the height of Boston-area construction activity.

builder and the designer, such as estimating cost of the systems before they were fully designed, determining the methods of fabrication and field assembly, and estimating the amount of time it would take to build components in the field. Since early estimates are normally based on historical models not applicable to this project, Skanska staff had to rely largely on their own understanding of the intent of the final design. In some cases, they involved subcontractors early to help craft these determinations. For the exterior cladding, for instance, a request for proposal to hire the subcontractor, based on performance criteria, preceded the completion of the construction documents. The Institute was essentially asking Skanska to hire a subcontractor to help with the detail design of this system, a very unusual arrangement that required a role change for Skanska as well as for the subcontractor.

One of the bigger challenges was finding tradespeople who were willing to guarantee their price to do the work. At the time of bidding,

the Boston labor market was tight: the largest public works project in the United States—the Big Dig, an underground rerouting of Boston's Central Artery—was in full swing, the economy was booming, and the dot-com industry was building facilities fueled by the enormous amount of available venture capital. The economic conditions made contractors choosy about the work they took on. On top of these external factors, the contractors bidding on the project needed to be sufficiently savvy to meet the technical challenges of costing, fabricating, and ultimately building the complex design.

Skanska needed to convince these tradespeople that the Stata Center was the right project for them. Since all parties had influence and relationships with the specialty-subcontractor industry, the final bid list was developed among the architect, the builder, and the Institute.

But even with this very select list, MIT and Skanska were concerned that the perception of risk would drive prices up. Gehry Partners was committed to finding ways

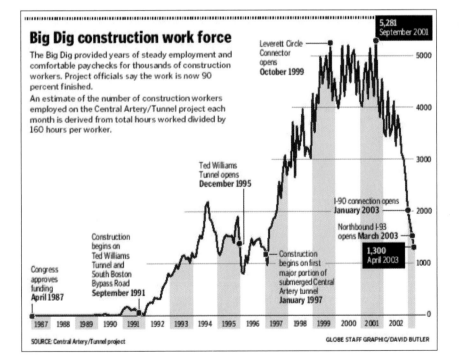

Big Dig construction work force

The Big Dig provided years of steady employment and comfortable paychecks for thousands of construction workers. Project officials say the work is now 90 percent finished.
An estimate of the number of construction workers employed on the Central Artery/Tunnel project each month is derived from total hours worked divided by 160 hours per worker.

Leverett Circle Connector opens October 1999

5,281 September 2001

5000

Ted Williams Tunnel opens December 1995

4000

3000

I-90 connection opens January 2003 — 2000

Northbound I-93 opens March 2003

Construction begins on Ted Williams Tunnel and South Boston Bypass Road September 1991

Congress approves funding April 1987

Construction begins on first major portion of submerged Central Artery tunnel January 1997

1,300 April 2003

1000

0

1987 1988 1989 1990 1991 1992 1993 1994 1995 1996 1997 1998 1999 2000 2001 2002

SOURCE: Central Artery/Tunnel project

GLOBE STAFF GRAPHIC/DAVID BUTLER

to explain the design and demystify the details as part of procuring bids from specialty subcontractors. The larger-scale model of the building was brought to Cambridge, full-scale mock-ups were installed at MIT, and smaller-scale models were assembled in California. Three-dimensional computer models showed how the different assemblies were connected. At design presentations for interested specialty subcontractors, designers from Gehry's office explained the intent of the design as well as the details; representatives of Skanska discussed their plan for organizing and managing the site over time; a 4-D model, consisting of the 3-D CATIA model overlaid with the schedule, clarified this process. These methods helped control the perception of risk. In addition, Skanska sent two of its engineers to California to be trained on the CATIA system and then purchased two stations for the site trailer. With this training and software in hand, the engineers were able to help the subcontractors with questions both during the bidding process and after award.

At the time of bidding, Skanska sent the construction documents to a number of companies in each trade—mechanical, electrical, steel, brick, and so on. At the end of that process, Skanska gave the Institute a guaranteed maximum price (GMP) for completion of the work as detailed on the construction documents. The GMP comprised the cost for the subcontractors' direct work, a contingency for unforeseen conditions, cost for indirect work (called "general conditions"), and an agreed-upon fee. From this point, Skanska was responsible for accomplishing what Gehry's staff had conceived. The weight of the work now shifted.

During the course of construction, the builder employs various

methods to accomplish the work detailed in the construction documents. Just as a builder would not tell an architect how to design the building, the designer will not tell the contractor how to build it. And just as a designer can be innovative in the way the building is conceived and detailed, the builder's processes can also be inventive. Field-designed tools and site-engineered solutions are involved in almost all aspects of building. As long as the outcome achieves the stated design goals, these tools and solutions remain under the builder's control.

The components of a building project are material, equipment, and labor. The architect specifies the material and its assembly. The builder typically specifies the

Colorful hand-drawn overlays of shop drawings (left) oriented the different tradespeople to the work under their specific contract.

Frequent site visits by senior faculty and administrators helped to demystify the construction process for them. At right, project director Nancy Joyce orients a group of visitors prior to leading a tour.

Chris Kelley, one of the superintendents on the job, went through twenty sketchbooks like those shown here. These books were used on site to take notes and sketch out solutions to site-specific means-and-methods problems. When design details needed to be resolved, Chris sent photographs of his sketches to the architect for approval. Many details on site can be traced back to these small sketchbooks.

equipment and labor needed to fabricate and install the material. Before the fabrication process begins, a formal, documented series of communications is held, at which the architect ensures that the builder understands the intent of the construction documents. This "discussion" takes place in the form of shop drawings and other submittals. The shop drawings, which are prepared by the specialty subcontractors, highlight exact details of how the material will be assembled. These drawings specify materials as specific as the type and size of

bolts. Since there is often more than one way to accomplish the goals of the design, the specialty subcontractor, who is in the best position to understand the most economical and efficient method of accomplishing those goals, normally controls this level of detail. Gehry Partners has learned to rely on the expertise these specialists bring to their work and, in some cases, has engaged a specialty subcontractor early in the design process to assist in detailing how the system goes together. Here Gehry's office diverges from traditional architectural practice.

In a traditional set of construction documents, many details are standard—used in other buildings and tested over time. Therefore, both the designer and the builder are familiar with the assembly and can predict how it will look, how much it will cost, and the amount of time it will take to install. Many architects also incorporate standard manufacturer's details, which have been tested in a controlled environment, in the design documents. Environmental conditions are mod-

eled and tolerances are tested against them. By specifying the material and assembly in the documents, architects can be sure that the system will stand up under stated tested conditions. In turn, the manufacturer recommends a specific method of installation for a particular product and often provides a list of certified trained installers. As long as the builder follows the recommendations for installation, the manufacturer will warrant the product.

Although Gehry Partners has developed a library of details and also uses manufacturers' details for some assemblies, much of their work is still far ahead of most standard ways of building. The firm is committed to finding and experimenting with computer technology and material science that can bring architecture to a new level. Each project is a new opportunity to push this goal forward, and this focus gives the builder a more integrated role in the entire process. Because neither tested standards of quality and performance nor a manufacturer's rulebook yet exist for many components, the team has to develop them together by using a number of methods, the most effective of which is the mock-up. For the Stata Center, exterior-skin components were mocked up at several off-site testing facilities. The glass was tested for watertightness and assembly details; a racking test examined the metal panels to ascertain their structural stability, while a thermal test did the same for thermal properties. Once details were worked out to meet the architect's performance criteria, components were released for fabrication.

Since the aim of all construction documents is to convey design intent to the workers in the field, it is critical that communication between architect and builder be ongoing, following agreed-upon rules. At the Stata Center project, two full-time architects were assigned to the construction site, where they handled day-to-day questions. Throughout the job, a Web-based project-management communication system served as the official communication tool for the entire team—architect, Institute, and contractor—all of whom logged on to the same site to send and receive all formal, recorded correspondence. The system helped ensure that the correspondence was clear and focused. Toward the end of the project, with time short and efficient decision making critical, a task team was formed to focus on specific field questions. On weekly site walks a representative from the architect, the field superintendent, and a project engineer tackled assembly details and design questions early on so that it was possible to keep ahead of the progress in the field.

Much construction-related activity occurs before material arrives on site. Unlike the automotive industry or product manufacturing, for example, construction calls for very few off-the-shelf parts. Even standard products are usually built to order. Detailed engineering activities, fabrication and manufacturing, and shipping and storage all occur behind the scenes. By the time materials arrive on site, they have undergone a number of processes. Once on site, they become part of an assembly plan. The following sections highlight some of these key construction activities as they were incorporated into the building of the Stata Center.

Although CATIA software and three-dimensional surveying equipment reduced the quantity of paper plans on site, a need to refer to these more traditional documents still remained.

Excavation

A 5.3-Million-Cubic-Foot Hole

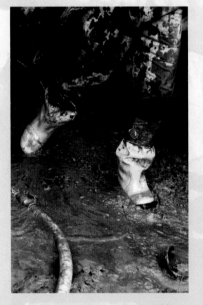

During the design of the Stata Center, MIT had applied to the City of Cambridge for a permit to expand an existing above-grade garage on a nearby site in order to replace the parking spaces that would be eliminated with the construction of the Center and to accommodate the new faculty, researchers, and graduate students who would move onto campus from rental space upon its completion. Since this expansion would direct additional traffic onto neighborhood streets, the city opposed it. In response, MIT proposed instead to include an underground parking garage as part of the construction of the Stata Center. The resulting increase in vehicles in this location discharges traffic onto nonresidential streets. Although more costly, this proposal made more sense as a long-term solution to parking needs and satisfied the city's concerns.

This decision led to a redesign of the foundation system, which now needed to accommodate the additional excavation for three underground

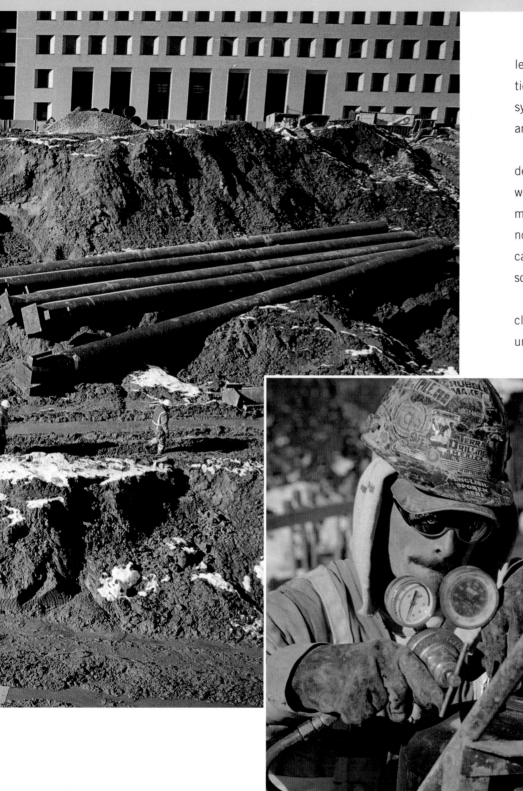

levels. Two decisions were made at this point: the type of permanent foundation needed to support the building over time and the temporary support system needed to hold back the soil and protect the surrounding structures and utilities during excavation.

A floating foundation was selected for the permanent foundation, designed so that the weight of the building would be balanced against the weight of the soil extracted from the site. When these weights are approximately equal, the stress on the soil beneath and around the excavation does not change. This method, used successfully in other buildings around the campus, was also cost effective. But a temporary method of holding back the soil during excavation was yet to be found.

The three-level excavation would now extend deep into layers of marine clay under the site. This soft, porous material is known for instability and unpredictable movement. To stabilize this soil during excavation, a concrete-reinforced-diaphragm (or slurry-wall) support system was recommended.

Many types of temporary walls are used to support deep excavations, and selection depends on specific needs. In this case, the slurry wall was used because the site has groundwater just nine feet below grade, and it is more watertight than other methods. Its construction is also quieter, which was important since the site is surrounded by research and teaching buildings. Finally, the slurry wall was chosen because it would provide a permanent underground wall for the three levels of underground spaces. Slurry-wall technology is relatively new to the Boston area, but through the extensive underground work during the Big Dig, many local contractors have become highly experienced in employing it.

With a 320-by-380-foot footprint, the open excavation was believed at the time to be the largest open hole ever in

Big machines worked in concert with one another, bailing soil to waiting trucks for removal to off-site landfills.

the history of Cambridge. Given the depth of the marine clay, a fair amount of risk was involved in the excavation, even with the best laid plans. The pressure from surrounding soil could make the open hole vulnerable to a cave-in. Compounding this risk was the weight of the existing buildings that hug the site and the placement of the utility conduit pipes that served the neighborhood.

The final design called for a thirty-inch-thick slurry-wall system, which would extend down seventy feet. Structural engineers ran several computer simulations, which showed that this system would provide enough rigidity to hold back the pressure exerted by the surrounding soil. Initially, the slurry wall acted as a simple cantilever, retaining the earth outside of the excavation. However, as the digging progressed downward, it became necessary to support the slurry wall

using three separate bracing methods. During the excavation, wall movement was closely monitored from many points, which were fixed with survey instrumentation embedded in the walls. The walls were expected to press inward no more than the safe distance of 1.5 inches; any movement beyond that could result in resettlement of adjacent buildings and utilities, which would have been costly and delayed the progress of excavation. But through very careful monitoring, quality control, and field engineering, the slurry wall and the subsequent excavation were completed in ten months, with no damage to adjacent buildings or utilities and, most important, no failures of the wall itself.

In the end, MIT got the desired garage—685 cars on two underground levels plus a shipping and receiving facility at the basement level. Besides meeting the city's criteria, it created the opportunity for MIT to develop more space for academic activities on the site of the former above-grade garage.

Subsurface Profile

Soil tests taken on the site through a series of 57 borings indicated groundwater at 9 feet, layers of organic material and sand in the first 30 feet, and marine clay in the next 80 feet. Bedrock was 140 feet below ground level in some areas. This information helped determine the type of permanent-foundation and temporary lateral-support systems needed for the building.

The material extracted from the borings was also tested for hazardous substances. Any material testing positive for hazards was separated during excavation, treated, and disposed of in a special off-site, lined landfill.

Bracing

To increase the load that these walls could carry and to ensure their vertical stability, tieback rods were added. Three levels of these long, woven-steel rods, some as long as one hundred feet, were

This geotechnical engineer's section denotes the areas where test borings were dug. The results of the test created a subsurface-soil profile that helped establish the type of foundation system needed.

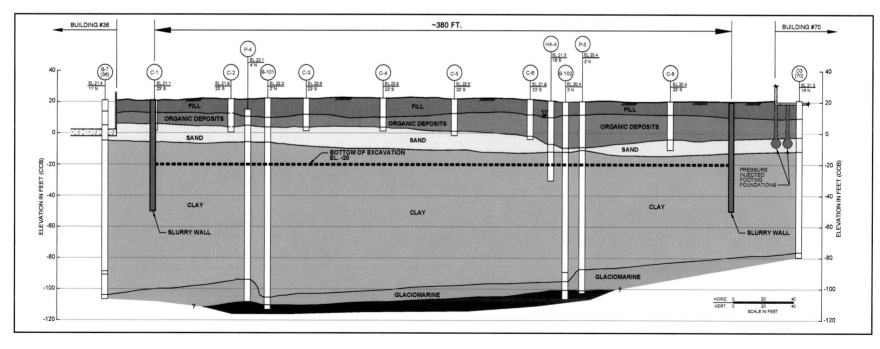

As the soil was removed and the hole deepened, bracing for the slurry wall was put in place. Bracing consisted of three levels of tiebacks on three sides, two levels of corner bracing on all four sides, and two levels of rakers on the north side.

spaced five feet apart horizontally and eleven feet apart vertically. What are essentially underground guylines were driven through presleeved, downward-slanted holes and then sealed into the ground with a rough grout mixture pumped into a PVC tube that was installed with the metal rod. The grout,

which settles at the bottom in a ball, creates tension on the tieback. Once cured into position and secured with a welded cap, each rod is pressure tested to guarantee that the grout and the welds are holding taut. This post-tensioning ensures that each tieback provides the necessary support for the wall.

Supplementary methods involved cross-bracing at the corners and internal bracing at the edge of the public street. Two levels of temporary beams, situated at ten feet and thirty feet below grade, designed to hold back the additional loads, were positioned at each of the four corners of the excavation. On the street side, two levels of preloaded steel tubes called rakers were installed, also at ten feet and thirty feet below grade.

Tiebacks could have been used on the street side as well, but the city was concerned that installation under the street would affect its stability. Rakers require support within the footprint of the excavation, so a soil berm supporting the north wall had to be left until a supporting slab at final grade was poured to accept the load of the raker.

Once the floors of the garage were able to support the outer foundation walls, the cross-bracing and the rakers were removed. The post-tensioning on the tiebacks was released but the tiebacks themselves were left in place.

Digging the Hole

With the diaphragm wall in place, the workers were able to start the actual excavation of the soil. In all, two hundred thousand cubic yards of soil were removed from the site amounting to ten thousand truckloads over seven months. The sequence of soil removal took into account the need to treat some of the soil separately. Soil was first removed along three sides of the site's perimeter, which allowed for installation of tiebacks. The middle of the site was left unexcavated until later in order to minimize destabilization of the surrounding areas. Soil was also left against the north wall until rakers were installed. Those areas identified as hazardous by test borings had to be removed in a specified manner and kept separate from the remaining excavated soil.

Slurry Wall Construction

At an average size of 25 by 2.5 by 70 feet each, sixty-nine slurry-wall panels were installed in a picket-fence arrangement to minimize stress from the surrounding soil.

The site was cleared of all utilities and other obstructions (top). A ten-foot-deep pre-excavation pit was dug around the entire perimeter. Since utilities are normally found within ten feet of grade, this ensured that none was missed. Inside this pit, at five feet below grade, a light concrete slab was installed to create a flat surface and a foundation for concrete guide walls.

These guide walls (center) align the clamshell digger and the reinforcing cage parallel with the trench.

As excavation for each wall panel proceeded, a slurry mixture—bentonite and water, which is heavy enough to hold back soil but sufficiently liquid to be pumped out when displaced by concrete—was pumped in (bottom). A slurry plant was erected on site and the slurry pumped to specific locations by a system of ground-laid pipes.

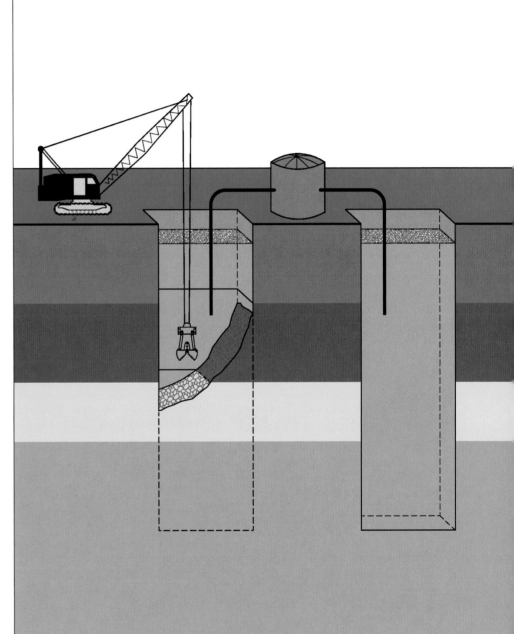

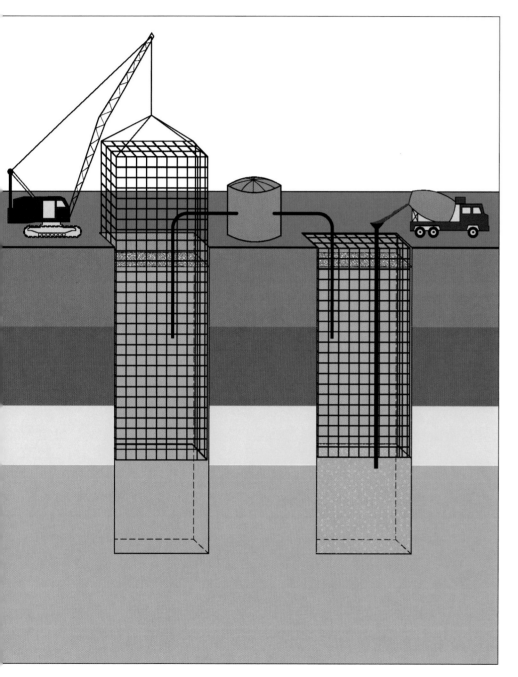

While one crew digs the hole, another assembles the reinforcing cage (top). Once assembled, the cage is moved into position.

Before the cage is placed, a steel keyway (center) is lowered on each side of the primary panels. This keyway provides a notch that then ties into the next panel when it is poured. The keyway also acts as a vertical guide for the cage as it is lowered.

Once the cage is secure, concrete is pumped in and the slurry pumped out (bottom). The displaced slurry is sent back to the on-site plant, filtered, and reused. The keyways are also removed and reused.

Throughout the excavation, the walls were continually measured for movement to ensure that they were successfully resisting the pressure exerted by the surrounding soil. The engineers devised a "movement mitigation" plan that allowed up to 1.5 inches of lateral shift in the newly formed walls. After about thirty feet of soil, measured vertically from the top of the slurry wall, had been removed, readings on the south wall, adjacent to the Alumni Pool, and on the west wall, adja-

cent to Building 26, showed inward movements rapidly reaching the specified limits. To offset the risk, the builders installed grade beams —three feet wide, five feet deep, and one hundred feet long—under the foundation slab to counteract the movement. This procedure slowed down the movement sufficiently to permit excavation to continue safely.

Near the end of the excavation, outward movement was detected on the north wall near the street, where

the internal rakers had been installed. Cracks in the sidewalk and the concrete-supporting footing were the first indications of this problem. A close examination of the rakers themselves revealed that they had expanded in the summer heat, which was causing them to exert force at both ends. The builder installed thermal blankets to insulate them. The tubes cooled and their expansion abated.

Four different monitoring devices were used to measure movement and stress. Eleven vertical tubes were installed in the diaphragm wall. As each level of earth was removed from the hole, an inclinometer probe was sent through one or more tubes to measure movement at intervals along their length. Since the tube ends were fixed to bedrock, they provided a zero-movement reference point. In addition to wall movement itself, it was crucial to measure movement of adjacent structures. In all, 125 settlement points—most on surrounding buildings but some along the adjacent public street—were installed to detect settling or heaving. Twelve vibrating-wire

piezometers measured changes in the groundwater pressure, and five extensometers measured movement within the soil layers below and outside the excavation.

Taken together, these four devices served as an early-warning system for unpredicted stresses. For example, this system detected the movements along the south wall early enough to allow preventive action. Data were collected through computer readouts or visual observation. In the end, even though the slurry wall moved in some areas outside the limits originally set up, preventive measures assured that no surrounding structures or streets were damaged.

Surveyors (top) kept close watch on the instrumentation that provided early warning of movement during the excavation process. Rakers along the north wall (bottom) tied into the slab at one end and the slurry wall at the other. Thermal blankets cooled down the rakers, which had heated and expanded in the August sun.

facing page:
Cross-bracing beams were welded in place (left). After the slurry wall was complete and enough of the permanent building structure was in place to provide lateral support, these cross-braces were sheared off and removed.

Clay is a fluid material (right), making for tough footing even on the sunniest of days.

87

Concrete

One Truck a Minute

The cast-in-place concrete structure of the Stata Center weighs in at 120,000 tons, represents 85 percent of the total weight of the building, and accounts for 20 percent of its cost. It constitutes the foundation, the floor slabs, the columns, the beams, and the roof. Because the undersides of the floor slabs and the columns are exposed, they also serve as finished surfaces. Twenty-four months—almost half the length of time required for the entire job—were spent pouring concrete. In the end, 80,000 cubic yards were poured, 60 percent of which is underground.

Concrete is an engineered material that combines natural ingredients to form a rocklike mass. The basic ingredients are cement, water, and aggregates. Cement is made up of a combination of limestone, clay, and sand that has been blended and ground into fine particles, heated to trigger a chemical reaction, and then finally ground into gray powder called portland cement, which is shipped in bulk to batching plants. There it is mixed with water and aggregate (gravel and crushed stone) in ratios specified by the designer. This mix determines the ultimate strength of the concrete. The water hydrates the cement

and provides mobility, which allows the concrete to be formed. The cement in its hydrated state binds the aggregate into a homogeneous mass. Upon shipment from the batching plant, concrete has a limited time to get to the job site before it starts to harden. In the case of the Stata Center, ninety minutes was the outside time limit, which meant that batching plants had to be local.

By the time the concrete arrived on site, much preparation had already taken place. Carpenters had assembled the formwork (or molds), electricians had snaked embedded conduit through reinforcing steel cages, plumbers had laid embedded pipes, and ironworkers had tied the reinforcing steel. Concrete is strong in compression but weak in tension, so reinforcing steel rods were added to provide tensile strength. The steel rods arrived on site cut and bent, with each bar marked and individually bundled. At the site, tying wires were used to join the rods by hand to form reinforcement cages inside the appropriate formwork.

When the cages were complete and the conduit and pipes in place, the concrete was poured around the steel rods. Principally, concrete was moved from the truck by means of pumps; when the reach was too far for the pump, wide, flat buckets moved by cranes were used to bridge the gap. As the concrete was pumped off the truck, it was tested for consistency through a slump test and for compressive strength through a cylinder test—four cylinders per one hundred yards were pulled. Once in place, the concrete was vibrated to ensure that it fully surrounded the reinforcing rods and filled the formwork completely, leaving no voids or excess air. Then it was smoothed to a level finish. The formwork was removed after the concrete had reached about 75 percent of its strength, which usually occurred within twenty-four hours, although in some cases it remained in place up to seven days. The formwork was then moved around site to be used again and again. The columns that

One of the unique elements was the skylight above the fitness center (top). Each of the formwork panels had to be individually constructed, using coordinates based on the CATIA model.

The engineered-formwork system (bottom) enabled the concrete subcontractor to quickly assemble the necessary shapes for the concrete floors. Once the formwork was in place, the reinforcing rods were assembled and the concrete was poured.

pages 88–89:
Pump trucks deliver concrete to the bottom of the hole, where the material is spread out to form a flat slab. When the reach is too far for the trucks, large flat buckets filled with concrete are moved by cranes to the required locations. The vertical steel reinforcing rods mark the location of the columns.

were part of the formwork system also acted as temporary supports for the concrete slabs until they were fully cured, which required approximately twenty-eight days. In a neat maneuver, the forms themselves could be removed without disturbing the structural supports.

Since the subcontractor had no experience with the CATIA three-dimensional software, the scope of the concrete work was documented entirely on two-dimensional drawings. However, three-dimensional drawings were also created to calculate volumes and to locate where the formwork would be placed in the field.

Formwork

The subcontractor used the PERI System, an engineered-formwork and temporary-support system from Germany, to form the concrete slabs, wall panels, beams, and columns. A panel-wall formwork, along with climbing brackets, was used to build the concrete walls, while an aluminum-slab formwork system was used to create the various ceiling heights and slab thicknesses.

Standardized column formwork was used when possible to form up the many columns. All these systems were supplemented with customized parts to accommodate the unique elements of the structure.

Forming the slabs encompassed the majority of the job. It was accomplished by using a system of reusable panels, beams, and posts. The posts—aluminum columns that allowed continuous adjustment to suit any ceiling height—enabled early stripping of the panels and beams comprising the formwork system, while the posts themselves stayed in place, acting as temporary shoring devices until the concrete was cured. This versatile system minimized the amount of materials that had to be brought on site and made it possible for every component to be handled by a single person.

Three stories below grade and nine stories above were structured principally in reinforced concrete. A combination of standard engineered forms and custom site-built forms were employed to establish the shapes.

Schedule and Logistics

A concrete pour must be continuous. To ensure that sufficient concrete was available, many of the larger pours were scheduled for Saturdays. For example, the foundation slab involved nine separate pours; one of the largest required thirty-six hundred cubic yards of concrete, representing twenty-four thousand square feet of floor area. Each concrete truck holds ten cubic yards.

Therefore the logistics entailed ensuring that the plants had enough concrete available, getting a sufficient number of trucks to the site, and efficiently unloading each truck during the ninety-minute period when the concrete was viable—very tight scheduling and planning, to be sure. In the end, for this pour six hundred cubic yards arrived on site per hour, the equivalent of one truck per minute.

Rebar

While concrete is a great material for resisting compressive loads, it does not do well under tension. Steel rods called rebar—some up to three inches in diameter—are assembled into cages, which gives concrete the tensile strength it lacks. These steel rods are ribbed to allow better bonding with the concrete. With its abundance of reinforcing steel, the placing of the concrete required special care to ensure that the concrete fitted around the rebar.

The steel rods came to the site individually cut and bent and packaged into bundles with identifying tags that corresponded to layout drawings. The reinforcing-steel fabricator used hand drawings below grade, then switched to AutoCAD for above-grade work. The assembly of the cages involved the very labor-intensive job of tying individual rods with wire. The assembly employed spacers and was welded at points to ensure that it retained its shape during the concrete pour.

The densely packed reinforcing rods made it challenging to ensure that the concrete was evenly distributed.

facing page:
To counteract the weight of the building above, the lowest level of the concrete pour, the foundation slab (left), was made four feet thick. Before the pour and after the installation of the reinforcing rods, electrical and data conduits and pipe runs for plumbing were woven among the rods.

The logistics of maintaining a continuous flow of trucks from the concrete plant and onto the campus made Saturday a favorite day for the big pours (right).

93

Building the Stata Center posed the particular challenge of positioning the different materials on site. For a traditional building with rectangular walls, a two-dimensional floor plan and elevations, along with standard surveying tools, would give the contractor enough information to locate points on site. On this project, with its oval shapes at the slab edges, twisting and sloping columns and walls, and deep beams at varying heights, a three-dimensional computer model along with a computer-ized three-dimensional surveying tool were needed to give the contractor the information needed to position the slabs, walls, and columns.

That technology exists in the form of a digitally linked, three-dimensional survey system called Total Station. To set up this system, the contractor first establishes control points off surrounding buildings. Using points established previously by MIT, the contractor then added more. Six prisms set on surrounding buildings reflected a laser sent from

a robotic surveying station, which calculated distances by measuring how long it took the light to travel to the prisms and back. By using the multiple points, the robotic station determined its own position. From there, with the help of a handheld survey device, and referring to the three-dimensional CAD drawings, the contractor was able to level and grade the site accurately and to align and position the slab, columns, and beams. Before the building was closed up, obscuring the prisms from view, the contractor

"It's not just how and when, it's where."

—Scott McKenzie, surveying engineer

established local control points so that lines of sight could be maintained continuously.

facing page:

From many vantage points, surveyors are able to locate desired coordinates by sighting on known points (left). Many tools come together to help locate needed points. Plans are drawn to scale over a thirty-foot grid, which is tied to a control point established for the entire project. Robotic surveying equipment (inset) ties into these plans and, with the help of handheld tools, any location on the plan can be found precisely on site (right).

below:

Despite the use of numerous high-tech tools, there is still a need for hand-drawn graphs and marked locators on site.

The graph (below) indicates the actual coordinates for the site markers' locations shown on the right-hand page.

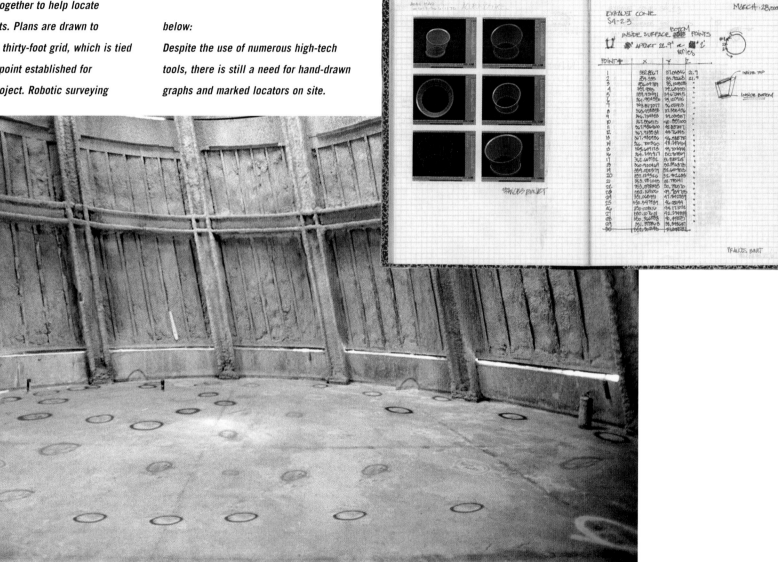

Structural Steel

2.6 Million Pounds of Steel

Steel is a relatively new material, arriving on the construction scene in the late nineteenth century. A manufactured material, it is made by melting iron ore with limestone and coke at high temperatures. This process removes most of the impurities and leaves molten iron (pig iron), which is mixed with lime in a furnace to remove the remainder of the impurities, known as slag, and then cast into beams that, by being run through a series of rollers, are shaped into the desired form. The structural engineer designates the shapes, sizes, and weights of the members required. Through a series of detailed drawings, the fabricator determines exactly how each piece will be made, its precise dimensions, and how it will connect to other members.

For the Stata Center, this shop-drawing process was accomplished through a combination of high-tech computer translations and low-tech drawings made by hand. Originally, the intent was to detail all the shop drawings

electronically, thereby achieving a paperless transfer from the engineer's desk to the fabricator's shop. As it turned out, some of the more complex elements were more efficiently produced by hand, and with schedules always at issue, these elements were sent out to steel detailers in Rhode Island, Massachusetts, and Maine.

The structural steel that forms the elements on the Stata Center's fourth and fifth levels and on some of the upper areas of the towers was fabricated both in Rhode Island and Canada. Full-size templates were devised to help position the bolt holes; connection devices, such as angles and base plates, were cut and numbered; and beams were cut to size, bent to the specified radius, and punched for bolt holes or prepared for welding. Once the fabrication was completed, the members were bundled for shipment.

Once the materials arrived on site, ironworkers started the installation process. Two 175-foot tower cranes helped hoist the steel into place. Surveyors, hired by the steel erector, located the position of the steel and checked the levels and the elevations as the erectors assembled the structural frames. The main steel members on each element were placed in an efficient sequence: first, the anchor plates were positioned; then the members were hoisted into place; and finally, connections were bolted and/or welded. Bolting is used for members that need to resist only sheer forces. Welding becomes necessary when the member also has to resist twisting forces. Sometimes a member is both bolted and welded. After the initial placement, however, a longer period of adjusting and welding secondary members took place—sometimes lasting for weeks. The secondary members made up the difference between the structurally necessary shape and the shape needed to support the metal panels or the brick that made up the final exterior closure.

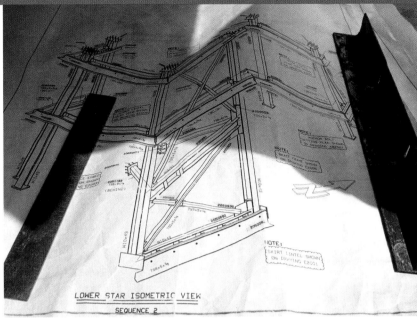

LOWER STAR ISOMETRIC VIEW
SEQUENCE 2

Curved-steel members (above, left) made up the structural base for the interior catwalks at each end of the Student Street.

Shop drawings (above, right) were used in the field to identify the location of the various steel members and the sequence of their installation.

The amount of staging required at any one time (right) necessitated careful sequencing of installation to allow for movement of workers and material.

pages 96–97:
As each piece of steel is lowered into position, it is guided by a worker holding a tagline.

Usually the surveyors come in once or twice and that's it. On Stata, we have survey crews here constantly because everything is leaning.

A lone welder atop Kiva makes some of the final connections of the primary steel members.

—*Rick Souza, Capco Steel*

Because a fire in a building can easily reach temperatures sufficiently hot to deform steel, building codes require that the steel be protected by fire-resistant material (left). In areas where the steel will be covered with a finished material such as drywall or wood paneling, the fireproof material is a sprayed-on, lightweight cementitious coating. This forms a passive fire-protective surface that insulates the steel from the effects of a fire and ensures that the steel will not reach temperatures sufficiently high to cause its collapse.

Wherever they will be exposed to the weather, steel members are coated with zinc—or galvanized (right and far right)—which prevents the steel from rusting. In addition, Gehry Partners required galvanization of all steel members that will be exposed to view.

When placing the steel members on anchor points, workers use hand signals (above) to communicate with the crane operator, whose job it is to support and position the member according to the hand directions.

At right, the contrast can be seen between steel used in an exterior application— in this case the support for a glass skylight —and steel used internally, which is coated with fireproofing and protected from the weather by metal panels.

For the Nose, the interior of the structural frame is left exposed; the finish plaster surfaces are built behind the frame. This is the one place in the building where researchers will be able to see the primary steel in full view. Steel members are pure engineered systems and have not been altered for architectural reasons. This means that member sizes may not be consistent along a rib, that the radius is made up of smaller asymmetrical arcs, and that a welded connection may be sitting next to a bolted connection. However, the connections have been cleanly executed, and the fireproofing is sprayed on with a smooth finish. This intumescent coating works by expanding when heated, which thermally insulates the steel and resists further fire damage. It also serves as the base for finished painting. Generations of engineers working in the lab can look around and reverse engineer the system to calculate the structural loads—a fun occupation for those downtimes.

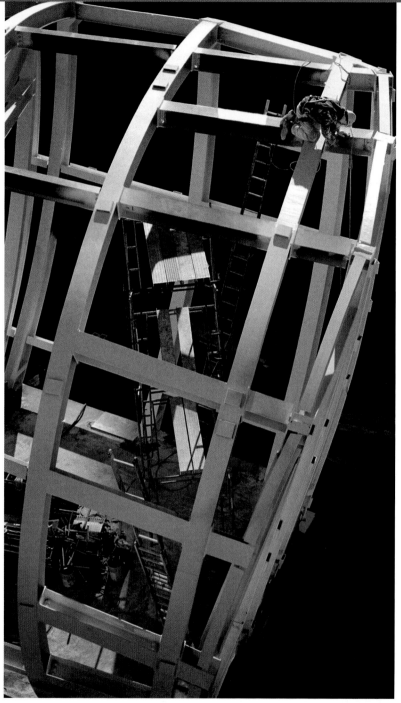

The steel for the Nose is protected by a smooth, sprayed-on fireproof coating that dries to a pinkish color, giving the frame the look of dinosaur bones. This coating was applied in layers and dried smooth, allowing the interior steel framing to be exposed. The prefabricated panels will be covered with a mirrored-finish stainless steel.

One Million Bricks

Bricks used in the construction of the Stata Center were installed by hand, one brick at a time. This task was among the last of a long line of preparatory steps.

The bricks came from large deposits of clay in the soil of southern Alberta and Saskatchewan, in western Canada. Typically, in order to obtain the properties and colors the architects required, two to six different clays were mixed. The mined clay was stockpiled and allowed to weather for one year, during which it was tested for mineral content, correct color, and other physical properties. After that year, the clay was crushed, ground, screened for impurities, and stored in bins at the plant.

The production cycle started with passing the ground clay through a mill, where it was mixed with water and extruded through a rectangular tube, then wire-cut into standard lengths. These individual bricks were then put in a kiln and dried. While they were on the drying rack, brick samples were randomly removed to track color consistency within the production run and to compare them to samples from other runs. Concurrently, an ultrasonic tester verified

that the density of the sample fired brick met the specified limits. Once the brick was approved for use by the manufacturer, mechanical arms unloaded it into trays, blending and sorting against a control sample. The bricks were then packaged by an automatic palletizing machine and shrink-wrapped for storage or shipping.

After considering brick from manufacturers in the United States and Canada, Frank Gehry chose this particular brick because it best met his requirements for color and texture. Although the architect approved the purchase based on a single-brick sample, he still needed to approve it in mock-up form before the order was placed. Once installed at the building site, this three-by-ten-foot sample panel verified the selection and demonstrated the aesthetic effect of the brick over a large area, in lighting conditions similar to those of the finished building. The architect and the Institute approved the sample for color, texture, the relationship of mortar and sealant color to the brick, and finally, the level of workmanship demonstrated by the brick installer. Upon approval of this sample, the builder placed the full order — one million bricks—with the manufacturer.

Once the brick started arriving on site, one more preparatory step was necessary before the masonry was fully approved. A full-scale mock-up was

built that showed all the components of the brick wall—the window system, relieving angles, the header/soffit at the window, and corner details. This dress rehearsal of the installation also demonstrated the waterproofing, mortar type and color, ties and anchors, flashing material, weep holes, and cavity-wall insulation. After a series of site meetings and discussions regarding acceptability of workmanship, the details of the weep holes, mortar, and tooling and cutting techniques, the architect approved the brick and the masons scheduled their crews.

Several different trades were involved in the erection of the exterior brick wall: glazers to install the windows, ironworkers to form the relieving angles, and drywall and concrete contractors to erect the walls behind the brick. Separate trades constructed the waterproofing and scaffolding systems, and of course, the masons installed the brick. Considerable coordination and cooperation among these trades were required to ensure success.

Strive for perfection; settle for excellence.

—Paul Theibalt, mason foreman

For the areas where sloped-plane walls and vertical walls tie into each other, much of the brick had to be cut by hand (above and below). To maintain control, the mason foreman assigned one master cutter, who designed custom jigs and performed all the cuts.

To support the weight of the brick, horizontal steel relieving angles were installed at intervals along the walls (below).

Waterproofing under the brick pavers has to hold up under the pressure of the walking surface above. A built-up waterproofing-membrane system, much like one on a roof, was used here (right).

Brick is used not only vertically but also horizontally—as a pedestrian walking surface, for example, or as a building ledge (above).

The first structural steel pieces to arrive on the site and to be erected into place were for the primary structure of the Star. But it would be eighteen months before the Star's last brick was laid. From start to finish, this was the longest construction duration of any for individual elements of the Center. Because of the compound angles on the building, the first challenge was to determine how to align the relieving angles, which were placed horizontally at intervals along the wall to support the brick. Since the angles needed to shed water, they had to be slanted. In order to align with other compound angles at their corners, which were different at each end, they had to slant along their length. Getting these angles right was crucial because they set the elevations for the bricks. And, since the bricks were required to align exactly as they were laid around the entire perimeter, there was no room for error. That issue was resolved nine months later and the masons

began work on their own challenge posed by the same compound angles at the corners. The angles formed at the corners were different at every row. This required every brick in that location to be cut differently than those in the same position in the rows above and below it. This was truly slow work that required a high degree of skill.

The winglike shapes of the roof (above) hint at the geometric complexity of the Star. The structural-steel elements, secondary steel, relieving angles, and concrete deck of the roofing slab had to be in place before the outer layers of waterproofing, insulation, and masonry could be installed.

Longer bricks (left), which had to be cut at eccentric angles, were used at the corners to provide structural and aesthetic integrity. These longer bricks ensured that each individual corner brick was

at least four inches long, no matter how eccentric the cut.

facing page:
The first piece of structural steel that was installed on site (left) was for the Star. The final element to be put in place in the configuration was the large window openings (right).

Metal

At the Stata Center, the exterior metal cladding is made primarily of stainless-steel panels. Developed in the early twentieth century by adding chromium and nickel to carbon steel, stainless steel is increasingly chosen by architects and engineers for a variety of uses because it is naturally resistant to corrosion. In the presence of air, an oxide layer, which inhibits corrosion, forms on the surface. This thin layer reinforces the natural color of the metal without compromising the metallic luster. Unlike rust, this film is stable and nonporous and adheres tightly to the surface. This means that the surface can be exposed without any applied coatings. It also is self-healing—if it is damaged, the layer re-forms, preventing further corrosion.

The material specified for the Stata Center is 316 alloy, which contains 17 percent chromium and 12 percent nickel. This combination gives the steel good pitting-corrosion resistance, a plus in a coastal environment.

The stainless steel arrived in coils from the mill shop in Pittsburgh to the fabrication plant in Kansas City; the coils were then cut and shaped as

detailed in the construction documents. Because the particular fabricator, Zahner, had done a lot of work for Gehry Partners, it had developed a seamless process for transferring the information directly from the documents to their fabrication machinery.

The metal panels formed an assembly; thermal insulation and waterproofing were applied directly to the panels before they arrived on site. Once in place on the building, the panels were joined with insulation. That joint was then taped and covered with waterproofing to protect the insulation and to allow thermal movement. Once this was done, the building was essentially weather-tight. The stainless-steel shingles applied over this assembly protect the waterproofing from ultraviolet light and damage and provide a finished surface. The shingles arrived on site protected by a blue plastic covering that was removed once the panels were in place.

Planning for the installation of the metal panels started early. When the concrete was being poured, steel inbeds—structural anchor points for the panels—were placed in the slab. Because this had to be done early in the process before the panels were completely designed, each inbed was designed to connect to a T-bolt and an aluminum angle called a candy cane. The candy cane provided the seat for the metal panel and the T-bolt moved in a slot in the inbed to allow adjustment.

The metal surfaces on the building establish at first a color and then a texture by which to define the forms. The color is derived from the material itself, which reflects light naturally, taking on a blue tint on bright, sunny days and a whitish-gray hue on overcast days. The surface of the stainless steel also was given a fine, radial texture known as "angel hair," which scatters reflected light, muting the reflection. Two patterns dominate the metal skin. The flat surface planes are 14-gauge thickness with panels sized at approximately twenty-four by sixty-nine inches. The panels are lined up vertically and staggered horizontally, giving an overall vertical appearance. The panels overlap but are not hemmed *pages 110–111:*

The window boxes that hold operable windows and all the metal panels were fabricated in Kansas City and shipped by truck to the site.

With so many sloping surfaces, much of the placing of the panels was done with cranes and the final installation of the stainless with lifts (right).

Steel structural anchors were cast into the concrete slabs to provide attachment points for the metal panels (below).

(meaning corners turned in). This creates a flat appearance with a thin visible edge. A concealed continuous clip makes the means of fastening invisible.

The other pattern is a 22-gauge-thick sheet of stainless steel, which is used on curved surfaces. The panels are hemmed over 180 degrees on all edges, employing a single lock seam. These panels again have no visible means of attachment. This thin skin and the interlocking edges distort the surface appearance. To provide a visual contrast and to highlight it as a special design feature, the Nose is clad with this gauge of steel but has a highly reflective finish.

You live it as you build it. That is a big part of succeeding on a job like this. I wake up at three in the morning, wondering if I checked some crazy detail.... That's the only way something like this can work.

—Dave Argus, curtain-wall foreman

The many ledges and soffits (left) make hanging the panels in these areas especially challenging. It takes more time because constant adjustments need to be made. Because the panels are all premade little room is left for error.

Other metals are used to develop the surfaces (above), including a custom color KYNAR paint over aluminum. This creates a contrast in color and lends reflectivity to the stainless surfaces. And to accentuate the entry canopies, corrugated titanium sheets are used. The titanium has a distinctive color and its appearance changes when viewed from different angles.

FOCUS The Skin

A sequence of steps (above, left to right) —from the full-scale mock-ups erected in South Boston, to final fabrication layouts, to on-site installation of the panels—culminated in the application of the metal skin, which resulted in the finished exterior metal-cladding system.

New England gets plenty of snow and ice, and sloping surfaces and jutting ledges create many opportunities for snow to build up. To offset this potential problem, the metal panels (right) are designed with oversized gutters that are heat traced, snow pins that break up the snow, and ice knives that break up any ice that forms.

A layered view of the finished metal surfaces (left) highlights the contrast between the flat-laying thicker-gauged metal and the subtle billow of the thinner-gauge metal.

Black waterproofing was applied over the metal panels and under the metal cladding (below). The finished surface was covered in blue plastic to protect it until all the work above was complete.

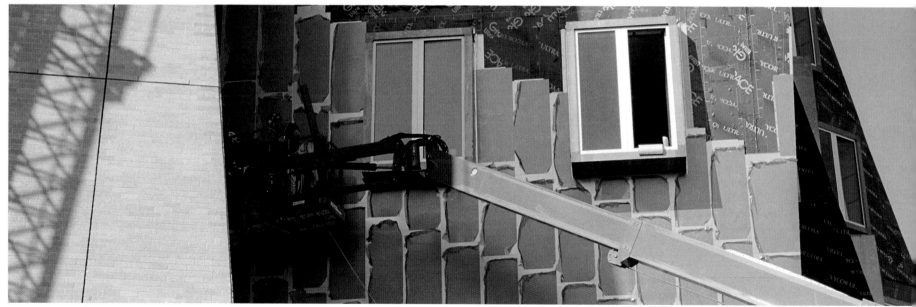

Glass

Natural glass, formed when certain minerals melt at extremely high temperatures and then cool rapidly, has existed since the beginning of time, but the first evidence of manufactured glass comes from Mesopotamia, around 3500 B.C. It was used at that time for beads and decorations. Its first use as a building material was in ancient Roman times when clear glass started to appear as glazing in important buildings in Alexandria around A.D. 100.

Throughout its history, various methods of producing glass have been employed, but the most common today is the float-glass process, developed in the 1950s. Glass is composed of more than 70 percent sand, which is mixed with soda ash, lime, and small amounts of aluminum and potassium oxide. These raw materials are heated to 1,500 degrees Celsius to produce a molten liquid, which flows in a continuous

ribbon from the furnace onto a bed of molten tin. Here it spreads and flattens and is drawn horizontally into the annealing chamber, where it is cooled further under controlled conditions to avoid internal stress. Once it has reached room temperature, it can be cut into specified sizes, then stacked and packaged for distribution.

Glass is used in several different ways at the Stata Center. It forms an exterior closure in a curtain-wall system and makes up individual operable windows and skylights. The aluminum and glass curtain-wall system is a non-load-bearing exterior wall. While made up of few components—glass, aluminum, and sealants—this system has to meet a complicated set of design criteria. The assembly has to control heat gain from sunlight, keep out moisture and air, resist wind, adjust to movement, and act as an acoustic separation.

Before the wall at the Stata Center was fabricated, it went through a series of tests to make sure that it would keep out moisture and air while resisting local wind forces and snow loads. During the tests, adjustments were made to the design, and through this iterative process of testing and redesign, the system satisfied the specified performance standards, allowing production to start.

BUILDING STATA

Flexible sealants (left) allow the curtain-wall assembly internal movement due to thermal changes—glass and metal react differently to temperature—while preventing passage of water and air through the system.

The operable windows (below) are double glazed—the inner glazing is tempered, and the outer glazing is tinted to reduce the passage of heat and prevent glare. The windows measure six by eight feet, and have mechanical stops that allow four-inch openings for fresh air but do not require an outside protective rail.

facing page:
Moving the glass panes required large suction cups attached to cables connected to the end of a crane arm.

pages 116–117:
At the top of the light courts (left), the glass curtain wall intersects at 90 degrees with large sheets of structural-glass skylight.

Stability, strength, and aesthetics were all considered in determining spacing of fasteners on mullions (center). At the skylight above the light courts, detailed coordination was necessary to make sprinkler lines and electrical conduits line up with existing structural grids (inset).

Because the curtain wall passes in front of the concrete floor slabs, a barrier had to be constructed between the two to prevent fire from spreading from story to story. These barriers were finalized in the field once the particular details of the curtain-wall attachment at the concrete slab could be seen along the complex geometry.

I don't know where I can go after this project. Where do you go after you've been to the moon? I can't see myself ever going back to another shoebox.... It's fun to be a part of something that will be talked about in engineering circles forever.

—*Dave Argus, curtain-wall foreman*

The challenge presented by an exterior glass system is to keep the rain, snow, and ice—along with air, unwanted natural light, and heat—from entering the building. This is complicated by the fact that precipitation driven by winds, sometimes at high velocity, will get into the building through any air leaks. In order to ensure that the curtain-wall system and the skylights proposed for the Stata Center would resist water and air penetration as well as perform structurally, a series of trials was prescribed.

At a testing facility in Miami, Florida, a full-scale model of the cladding system, two stories high and one bay wide, was erected. First, structural loading and air infil-

tration were tested by replicating the expected wind velocities and snow conditions that exist in the vicinity of the new Cambridge building. The assemblage was then tested for water leakage by subjecting it to two different conditions. First, a static air-pressure test modeled the air pressure differential that exists across the building wall. This pressure creates suction, moving moisture through any small opening from the exterior of the building, where higher air pressures exist. For the test, the assembly was wetted at a rate of five gallons per hour per square foot, re-creating the conditions of an average rainy day without excessive winds or downpour. In the second test, a dynamic water test, an aircraft engine and propeller drove water against the wall. Based on results of these tests, the design team modified the gasketing and end-condition details, the gutter, and the condensation drainage. Other concerns, such as determining the spacing and how many nuts and bolts would be used through the mullions, were finalized.

facing page:
Dave Lewis (left), the owner's construction representative, records results of flood testing from within the mock-up chamber.

Setting up for the testing procedures, the Miami site of the glass flood testing (facing page, right, and above) looks like an old Hollywood movie set, with a cartoonlike truck and an airplane engine-

propeller motor. The propeller is used to test water infiltration under high-wind conditions. Paul Hewins (inset), Skanska's project manager, observes the effects of the replicated wind conditions.

Six Million Cubic Feet

Well before the interior of the building was fully protected from the weather, the builder had begun the process of installing those elements that directly and visibly support the work that would go on inside upon completion. As early as the pouring of the concrete, accommodations were being made for interior systems. Conduits embedded in concrete slabs house the wires and cables for power, lights, and data. Cutouts in each floor's slab accommodate the vertical transportation of heating and air conditioning ductwork, plumbing pipes, and electrical cabling. At each floor, these systems branch off horizontally to specified locations.

Anchored directly to the concrete floor slab, this arrangement presented some challenges during construction. Pipes, conduits, and ducts had to be protected from continued construction activity temporarily until permanent

protection was put in place. This protection is a system of two-foot-square concrete floor tiles raised fourteen inches on pedestals. The decision about when sequentially to install this raised floor had to be weighed against the continued need for access beneath the tiles. In some instances, part of the raised floor was installed but critical junctures remained open until the last minute.

Once the exterior of the building was partially weather-tight, the builder was able to start installing partitions, which consisted of three different types: standard, full-height drywall partitions, custom-finished, full-height, exposed heavy metal–gauge studs; and partial-height plywood dividers. These three systems make up the basic language of the building. Most were installed after the raised floor was in place and they are anchored to this floor, thus leaving the space open underneath. However, for code and safety reasons, the full-height partitions in the computer machine rooms, biochemical labs, electric and tel-data closets, and the toilet rooms, were anchored directly to the concrete floor slab, which separates them from the surrounding areas.

Because the raised floor is removable, the finish must be removable as well. The most economical and versatile choice, carpet tiles, are used throughout the building. These tiles meet stringent environmental criteria and use an adhesive that will restick if the tile is pulled up. Holes were cut in the raised floor and the carpet tiles to accommodate under floor–mounted power and mechanical systems.

Other finishes include acoustical treatments and wood millwork. Although the ceilings were conceived as being exposed concrete, acoustical treatment was applied to them in various areas. For example, the lounges and some of the more ceremonial spaces have a troweled-on acoustic-plaster finish called Bauswaphon. This surface, principally used for ceilings but also applied to the wall surface in the Star, gives the clean look of smooth plaster but has sound-absorbing properties. However, the cost of the extensive labor required to install this material brought about its sparing use in the building. In the

125

Before the building is turned over to the owner, the builder reviews each space and creates a punchlist, which enumerates all the small-scale or touch-up work still to be completed. This process requires diligence on the part of the builder and is tied into the final payment made by the owner.

pages 124–125
Close to completion, many finish activities happen at once at the west end of the Student Street (center).

Temporary workstations, complete with task lighting (inset), provide the electrical subcontractor with a convenient place to do paperwork.

open labs, the Student Street, and conference rooms, acoustic panels were used instead. Perforated-wood paneling in the auditorium, classrooms, and the boardroom must perform acoustically as well. This paneling, used mostly on walls but also on the ceiling of the auditorium, has a sound absorbing–fabric backing. Other uses of wood in the building include corridor baseboards, sills and shelving in the offices, casework in the tea kitchens, and custom built-in furniture on the Student Street. As a special application, wood salvaged from the beams and columns of the demolished Building 20 is used as paneling and wood flooring in the fourth-floor pub and faculty dining room.

Three stages of completion show the auditorium's transformation from plain concrete box to wood-clad lecture hall with floating acoustic ceiling and high-end audio-visual systems.

Sloping columns are difficult to hide in straight walls. As a result, they appear in surprising places throughout the Stata Center, adding to the rich viewscapes but creating challenges for furniture placement.

Watching the interiors of the Stata Center come together was a journey of discovery. The simplicity and clarity of the finishes provide a backdrop for the dramatic geometry of the exterior. Partitions, interior glazing, and double-height spaces all frame unique and unexpected views throughout. The building wraps around itself, providing glimpses of architectural elements, working activity, or natural light. Like passing by a mirror quickly and catching sight of yourself, an instant of strange unfamiliarity precedes recognition. This "out of body" experience lends itself to contemplation, a pause in the daily routine. As the project developed, surprising views were unveiled one by one, as if in a slow-motion movie. No one knows each striking feature of the Center as intimately as the people who built it.

All the floor tile arrived on site at once and had to be stored prior to installation (left). Since each tile weighs forty pounds, the installer conferred with the structural engineer to ensure that the waiting tiles did not overstress the concrete floor.

The raised floor had to be in place before the partitions, which sit on top of it (below). Electrical, phone, and data cabling was distributed underneath the floor at a later date, however, so tiles in specific areas were removed to accommodate this work.

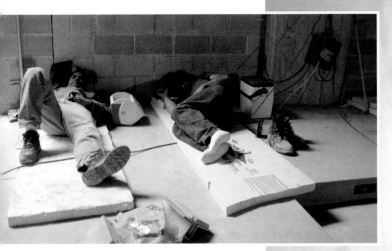

Insulation provides an easy surface for men resting on their break (above), some of whom leave home well before daylight to arrive at the jobsite by 6:00 AM.

Lengths of two-by-fours provide a ready table for communal dining (right).

The elevator (far right) was used by every worker at one time or another so it became an informal communication hub, with notices, posters, and off-the-cuff decorating schemes. During the Christmas season, for example, a homey touch was added with a tree and lights.

When members of the MIT research community move into the Stata Center, most people will consider them to be the first occupants. In fact, the first occupants of the building were the construction workers. These men and women spent eight—sometimes ten or twelve— hours a day working collaboratively or singly, eating, socializing, and taking rest breaks on site.

When most people go to work, they walk into a space with a prescribed means of navigation via stairs, elevators, and clearly marked passageways. There are conference rooms for meeting, offices for private work, kitchens for eating, and lounges for breaks. A construction

site is not like an office building. It does not provide ready-made spaces for any of these activities. It is open to the elements, and the work space changes every day. When the workers arrive on site, they have to define these areas for themselves, and they continually redefine them as the project evolves. Despite the transitory nature of this personal and team space, the result is sometimes surprisingly homey.

The clarity of the interior design was evident from the time that the concrete slabs were formed. Workers carved out pathways to move material, equipment, and personnel through the building. Although not marked in any way, these pathways were, in fact, the architects' intended circulation routes through the finished building. The Student Street, at ground level, became the main horizontal avenue of this construction activity. From there, ladders provided means of passing from floor to floor. Many were placed surprisingly close to where stairways were to be built. Up on the higher floors, traffic hugged the interior core in the same way that it does in the completed Stata Center.

The construction of a building is a magical thing, sometimes seemingly defying the laws of physics. Workers are able to stand in spaces that will never physically exist again. Hollow formwork initially defines a space, but once filled with concrete the form takes on a different character as a solid. Shafts that cut vertically through the building are eventually filled with ductwork and conduit, then covered with solid walls; but while the shafts are under construction, workers traverse them easily. Standing on a newly formed slab, the team saw views to the surrounding community unfettered by obstructions, revealing vistas that will never be seen in quite the same way once the walls are constructed. Temporary staging along the sides of the building provided similar vantage points. Walking through walls was an everyday event until the drywall was installed.

Ghostly footprints on ceilings, graffiti on steel beams, penciled instructions and calculations on columns and the back of drywall partitions all attest to the community of workers who inhabited the Stata Center first. Perhaps, the new occupants will feel their presence.

Afterword

Unlike the popes and potentates who were the great architectural patrons of the past, modern universities do not present themselves as singular architectural clients. Instead, they are complex and contentious assemblages of powerful corporation members, presidents, provosts, treasurers and investment committees, deans and department heads representing the interests of their particular academic constituencies, alumni, donors, client committees, professional advisors, articulate and persuasive faculty members debating fundamental ideological and philosophical issues, students whose voices demand witness, local community groups representing neighborhood interests and in-house staff responsible for keeping projects on time and on budget. The success of Frank Gehry's design for the Stata Center can be measured by the breadth and generosity of its attention to these diverse and sometimes contradictory voices, the rigor of its refusal to provide over-simplified responses, and the vivid assurance with which it represents the social conditions and cultural contingencies of its particular time and place.

The straightforward management view of the project was that the space necessary for MIT's operations is essentially a commodity—not too different, really, from kilowatts of electric power or gigabytes of computer memory. You produce or acquire it at some cost per square foot, maintain and service your inventory of it for some yearly charge, and eventually dispose of it when it no longer pays its way. You measure arcane indices like net-to-gross ratios, laboratory versus non-laboratory space, and the percentage of the cost that you can recover from the Federal Government, to determine whether you are getting a good deal. You apply space standards for various classes of activities, and you benchmark your costs against those of other organizations. You prioritize space needs and seek optimal assignments of activities to locations. You compile ruthless value-engineering hit lists as you strain to meet budget targets. You go to the capital markets to finance construction and real estate acquisitions, and you worry about your debt-to-equity ratio. When you hear the word "architecture," you reach for your spreadsheet.

This perspective is realistic and appropriate enough, but in itself far from sufficient. The counterpoint is that, as a leading intellectual institution with a commitment to innovation in design and the visual arts, MIT carries a particular responsibility to conceive of construction projects more ambitiously—not just as the rational allocation of resources to achieve quantifiable management goals, but also as inventive, critical contributions to our evolving culture. To support anything less, as proponents were quick to point out when goals and priorities for Stata were debated, would be as scandalous a betrayal of the Institute's principles as the fostering of pedestrian scholarship or mediocre science. In the end, Gehry's brief—one particularly suited to his talents—was to produce a work of architecture that both functioned as an efficient, pragmatically organized research asset and imaginatively engaged its broader urban, social, and cultural contexts.

Among the most critical factors determining the character of an urban building is the nature of its participation in the ongoing formation of the city. At the very least, it should make its immediate neighborhood a more commodious and interesting place to be. More subtly, it should play its part in a collectively constructed fabric of meaning that unfolds and transforms itself across generations—evoking the narratives of the city's past, commenting upon its current condition, and expressing aspirations for its future. The Stata Center was built in a tough old industrial corner of Cambridge—down by the railway line, and about as far from the cozy Georgian (well, mostly fake-Georgian) of Harvard Square, and the mansions of Brattle Street, as you can get. Its materials of steel and brick, and its allusions to the forms of large-scale industrial installations, will provide permanent reminders of that era of Cambridge's development—most evidence of which is rapidly being removed, like an embarrassing old relative being shuffled off the scene, as the area transforms itself into the very model of a modern major info-, nano-, and biotech hotspot.

Vassar Street, on which the Stata Center fronts, began life as an industrial service street. Over the decades, MIT lined its south side with austere laboratory buildings that, by the 1990s, had massed into a forbidding wall stretching from Main Street to Massachusetts Avenue. Furthermore, the corner of Vassar and Main, which was potentially a connecting zone between the newly enlivened Kendall Square area to the southeast and Technology Square to the north, had become a grim tangle of decrepit

and uninviting architectural remnants. So the forms and circulation systems of Stata have been configured to repair these conditions and establish a sense of graceful urbanity. They provide a handsome and satisfying completion of the urban edge along the south side of Vassar Street, transform the corner of Vassar and Main into a lively link between the Kendall and Technology Square areas rather than a wasteland dividing them, and provide inviting paths into the campus from the communities to the northeast. In coordinated MIT projects, the north side of Vassar Street is being reshaped by Harry Ellenzweig's elegant steel and glass extensions to MIT's power plant complex, and by another fine laboratory building—a limestone-faced powerhouse of brain and cognitive science research by Charles Correa and Goody/Clancy. As appropriate to its new role as a circulation route serving major campus destinations, Vassar Street has been transformed from a campus "back road" into a tree-lined, pedestrian-welcoming and bicycle-friendly boulevard.

Within the context of the MIT campus itself, the Stata Center is a continuation of the well-established pattern of quadrangles and continuously connected internal corridors—the famous infinite corridor system that has characterized MIT's buildings since it was initiated with William Welles Bosworth's neoclassical Killian Court and Main Group in the early 1900s. Fortunately, however, in building its campus over the decades, MIT has never fallen into the trap of insisting on skin-deep stylistic unity (all columns and domes, collegiate gothic, or some-

thing of that sort) to anchor it at some idealized point in the past. Instead, it has encouraged critical reinterpretation of this underlying system with each new wave of construction. Eero Saarinen produced a mid-century, heroic modernist version on the west side of Massachusetts Avenue, with the pure geometry of the Kresge Auditorium and the Chapel answering to Bosworth's two great classical rotundas. I. M. Pei did it in sixties concrete, with a dramatic juxtaposition of horizontal and vertical monoliths, to create Eastman and McDermott

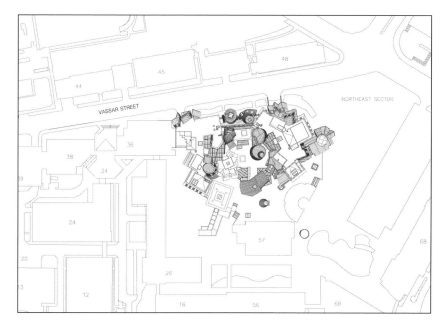

Courts directly to the south of Stata. In the eighties, for an odd-shaped court bounded by Romaldo Giurgola's Whitaker College and Health Services buildings, and Pei's Wiesner Building, the landscape artist Richard Fleischner did a postmodern polychrome-paved version. Now, for the new century, Frank Gehry has reinterpreted the theme once again.

As you approach from the heart of the campus to the south, you discover that curtain-walled, slab-sided, existing buildings provide crisp boundaries to Gehry's quadrangle on the east, south, and west. New construction along the Main Street boundary will eventually complete the enclosure. Stata rises to the north, along the Vassar Street edge. Two brick towers clasp irregular garden terraces that ascend, like a temple-studded Greek acropolis, from an amphitheater at the base. Since MIT is built on fill dumped into the wetlands of the Charles River, in a way that would surely be illegal today, this artificial mountain is the Institute's only vertical topography. But don't expect classical declamation in the theater—not

often, anyway; in a more demotic mode, it primarily provides a staging ground for the much-patronized lunch trucks to come and park each day. Purchase your falafel, then take it to your chosen elevation on the sunlight-washed steps.

These terraces rise up from the shadows that would otherwise gather, and the surrounding construction provides shelter from prevailing winds. The effect is to shift the microclimate of this special corner of the campus to a more hospitable latitude—a particularly welcome move in Boston's raw early spring and rapidly chilling fall.

The underpinnings of the terraces, together with the two flanking towers, contain a vast quantity of straightforward, flexible, pragmatically organized, and relatively inexpensive laboratory and office space. This teeming workspace is the building's intellectual and economic engine, and the justification for its existence. It is mostly a tissue of open research areas surrounded by clusters of offices, and it embodies a very specific vision of research communities and their dynamics

that grew out of intense, extended, probing discussions between the architect and the client group. This is architecture as inventive problem solving, in the service of social goals, under very tight constraints— the sort of work that established Gehry's early reputation in projects such as the Rouse Company Headquarters from the 1970s and the Loyola University Law School from the 1980s.

As is necessary and standard with modern laboratory space, Stata provides large floor plates, modularity, and the capacity for rapid reorganization in response to changing research goals and emerging intellectual agendas. In the latter part of the twentieth century, at MIT and other research universities, these requirements often found simplistic expression in huge, repetitive brutes of buildings that destroyed the human scale of campuses and their neighborhoods, and certainly contributed to the alienated spirit of campus communities in the sixties and seventies. But Gehry's design for Stata says hell no, we won't go— not with that program. It cleverly

exploits the fact that, when a building's mass grows very large, you can sculpt it without great loss of internal efficiency and flexibility. (When the area-to-perimeter ratio of a floor plate is large, a few kinks and bumps in its shape don't much matter.) And it breaks down the scale of the exterior surfaces with cascades of much smaller, highly sculptural, mostly metal-clad elements that house entrance areas, meeting and public spaces, important offices, and other of the building's more public functions. If you look at some sections, you can immediately see how a highly articulated, non-repetitive exterior has been skillfully grafted onto a straightforward, flexible interior reminiscent of the much-loved but worn-out Building 20 that previously occupied the site.

The sections also reveal a strategy of creating some large-scale, almost Piranesian interior spaces that cut like chasms, caverns, and canyons through the mountain. These bring daylight and long vistas, in many unexpected and beautiful ways, deep into the heart of the building. And their nooks and crannies create a variety of social spaces, informal workspaces, and places to escape with a book or coffee cup. The grandest of these spaces—the ground-level Student Street—is Stata's continuation of the infinite corridor system. But, unlike most other parts of that system, it is designed as a place in and of itself, not merely a highway taking you to someplace else.

According to a central dogma of design in the machine age, all this humanizing articulation and playful spatial variety are bad things. Architects should rigorously expunge it in the interests of modularity, repetition, and economies of scale—as, for example, in MIT's hair-raisingly single-minded Building 13. Anything else, as some of the Institute's hardliners will still passionately maintain, is an affront to the principles of parsimonious rationality that made MIT great. But times and technologies change. Today, the combination of three-dimensional digital modeling of designs, CAD/CAM fabrication, and digitally controlled on-site assembly processes makes the cost difference between repetitive and non-repetitive designs increasingly marginal; the aesthetic conventions of industrial modernism are no longer grounded in actual conditions of production. Frank Gehry, more successfully than any other architect of our time, has learned to shrug off the standard design assumptions of the recent past, and to exploit the emerging freedoms of the digital era. Stata continues a path-breaking exploration of digitally mediated construction possibilities that began with a fish-shaped pavilion on the Barcelona waterfront, and then pushed into astonishing new territory with the Bilbao Guggenheim Museum and the Disney Concert Hall.

The vocabulary of Stata's sculptural spaces and masses does not repeat the flowing spline curves, appropriated from ships and aircraft, of Bilbao and Disney. It is not as pure and abstract as the repertoire of cubes, cylinders, spheres, and cones of early modernism, nor as literally mimetic as the copybook of late-twentieth-century postmodernism in its moment of perilous flirtation with historicist pastiche and kitsch. Instead, it finds a way to be richly but ambiguously allusive. You can read in it the vivid gestures of the architect's hand—the rhythms of early sketches, and the forms of curved, folded, and crumpled paper from the first models. Foreshortened in the distance, the elevations suddenly seem like cubist canvases—particularly Fernand Léger's machine-obsessed renditions of bodies and cities. For architects, the declensions of sheetmetal shapes are an instruction manual in the new grammar of CAD/CAM construction. For photographers, the metal, glass, and masonry surfaces present complex and often breathtakingly beautiful, animated combinations of shading, shadows, and reflections.

For ideologically attuned urbanists, Stata's intricacies, surprises, and refusal of rigid system are (with a passing nod to Camillo Sitté) a standing rebuke to the Main Group's too-easy assumption of the architectural language of authoritarian power, as it was deployed from Versailles to Albert Speer. For those with a sense of humor, the elevations function like Web pages of hotlinks to objects in the surrounding environment; that slender, inverted cone, for example, is surely intended for the ice-cream-scoop radar dome on top of the Green Building. And for those who love Alvar Aalto's Baker House, Gehry's work is an homage to a great predecessor; compare, for example, the ways that the two masters handle the placement of regularly spaced, rectangular windows in curved and irregular walls.

Stata does not aspire to the classical virtues of unity and timelessness. Appropriately for a building that sits on the site of the legendary old Radiation Laboratory, it works, instead, like a giant transponder. You can ping your preoccupations, thoughts, and desires at it on different cultural wavelengths and get surprising and challenging messages back. For the complex, diverse, multicultural, sometimes contradictory community that MIT has become in the twenty-first century, this seems just about right.

—William J. Mitchell

Index

Note on the alphabet: Each letter of the alphabet used in this index is an object found on the site of the Stata Center during its construction.

Project Participants

a·g Licht
ABC Moving Services
Abs Consulting/EQE International
Acme Office Systems, Inc.
Acme Waterproofing
Advanced Signing, Inc.
Alleghany Flooring
American Plumbing & Heating Corp.
American Power Conversion Corp.
Andover Controls Corp.
Architectural Skylight Co., Inc.
Automation Solutions, Inc.
Babfar Equipment Rental
Back Bay Sign Company, Inc.
Baron Industries, Inc.
Bart-Lund Steel Services
Bay State Blackboard Co., Inc.
The Becht Corporation
Bloom South Flooring
Bonaco Company, Inc.
Brand Scaffold Rental & Erection
Bright Window Coverings, Inc.
Broadway Electrical Company
Campbell McCabe Inc.

J.C. Cannistraro & Co. Inc
Cannon Design
Capco Steel Corporation
Capital Precast
H. Carr & Sons, Inc.
CBI Consulting
Chapman Waterproofing Co., Inc.
Charrette Corporation
Chase Precast Corp.
The Cheviot Corp.
Cini Little
Circle Floors
Citadel Consulting
Columbia Steel
Component Assembly Systems, Inc.
Comtronics Corp
Consolidated Brick & Building Supplies, Inc.
Continental Bridge
Cox Engineering
Creative Pipe, Inc.
Crimson Tech
Cullinan Engineering
Diversified Project Management
Edifice Wrecks
Eggers Industries
Eidams Parking & Access Control
Electronic Engineers

Environmental Health & Engineering
Fairweather Site Furnishings
Figueras Seating
M.J. Flaherty Co.
Fleet Industrial Service, LLC
James W. Flett Co.
The Floor Sanders
FM Global-Northeast Field Engineering
Forms and Surfaces Company
Fox Associates
Front Line Cleaning
Fuller Associates, Inc.
G.P. Marketing
Gehry Partners, LLP
Grande Masonry
Greenheck Fan
Greenheck Louver
Haley & Aldrich
Hanscomb Associates
Hartford Roofing Co., Inc.
HB Communications
Hercules Steel Inc.
J.C. Higgins Corp.
Hung Associates
Hunnicutt Davis
IOI Inc.
ISI Internetworking

J.A.J. Company
Julian Crane & Equipment Corp.
K&K Acoustical Ceiling, Inc.
Keville Enterprises, Inc.
Kroll, Inc. Security Services Group
Lab Furniture Installation & Sales
Lanco Scaffolding, Inc.
LCN
Lerch Bates North America, Inc.
Jacob A. Licht, Inc.
Limbach Company, LLC
Longden Company, Inc.
Mac Systems
MacFarlane Steel Corp.
Mark-A-Lot, Inc.
Marr Riggins Company, Inc.
Marshall & Sons
John A. Martin & Associates, Inc.
Martin/Martin-Utah Inc.
Mass Electric Construction Co.
Bruce Mau Design
McCusker-Gill, Inc.
McKay, Conant, Brook Inc.
Media Systems Design Group
Mousseau Contract Flooring
NER Construction Management, Inc.
New England Finish Systems

New England Specialties
North American Woodworking
Judith Nitsch Engineering, Inc.
O'Leary & Associates
Olin Partnership
PACE Representatives
Paint Systems of New England, LLC
Pappas Company
John A. Penny & Co.
Planet Earth Playscapes
Polybois, Inc.
Port Morris Tile & Marble Corp.
Precast Specialties
Pro Cut
Q & W Associates, Inc.
Redi-Check
Ripman Lighting
Rolf Jensen & Associates, Inc.
Rowen William Davis Inc.
RSG Contracting Corp
S & F Concrete Contractors, Inc.
Save-On-Wall
Schirmer Engineering Co.
SEA Consultants, Inc.
Signworks
Silktown Roofing
Skanska USA Building, Inc.

Susan Skrupa Studio
Richard M. Sobol
Gordon H. Smith Corporation
Soep Painting Corp.
South Shore Millwork
Spaulding Brick Co., Inc.
Stanley Works
Steelco Chain Link Fence Co.
Gail Sullivan Associates, Inc.
Sullivan & McLaughlin
Terra Drilling Co., Inc.
Thompson & Lichtner Co. Inc.
Thyssen Dover Elevator
Tishman Construction Corp.
Tower Glass
Tractel, Ltd.
Trevi Icos Corp.
Valley Crest Landscape Development
R.G. Vanderweil Engineers, Inc.
Watch All, Inc.
Watertown Iron Works, Inc.
Weidlinger
The Welch Corp.
West Hartford Lock Co., Inc.
WoodCeilings
Worcester Air
Zahner/Karas Joint Venture

Edited by Brian D. Hotchkiss and designed by Peter M. Blaiwas for Vern Associates, Inc.

Production coordinated by Terry Lamoureux — Composition set in Trade Gothic by Folio Publishing Services

Printed on 100# Utopia Two Gloss Text and bound by Quebecor World, Kingsport, Tennessee